Touring Car
1997-1998 year

CONTENTS

THE OFFICIAL REVIEW OF THE AUTO TRADER RAC TOURING CAR CHAMPIONSHIP 1997

EDITOR ANDY HALLBERY **ART EDITOR** TIM SCOTT **EDITORIAL ASSISTANTS** NICK PHILLIPS, JONATHAN NOBLE, BRUCE JONES **DESIGNER** JOHN BLUNDELL **PHOTOGRAPHY** LAT, BOTHWELL PHOTOGRAPHIC, **ADDITIONAL PHOTOGRAPHY** MALCOLM GRIFFITHS, COLIN McMASTER **ASSOCIATE ART EDITOR** PETER CHARLES **PUBLISHER** MARTIN NOTT **PUBLISHING MANAGER** JULIAN DANIELS **SALES DIRECTOR** JOHN CHAMBERS **PUBLISHING DIRECTORS** PETER FOUBISTER, JEREMY VAUGHAN **MANAGING DIRECTOR** TONY SCHULP

TOURING CAR YEAR 1997-1998 IS AN AUTOSPORT SPECIAL PROJECT PUBLISHED BY HAYMARKET SPECIALIST PUBLICATIONS LTD, 38-42 HAMPTON ROAD, TEDDINGTON, MIDDX TW11 0JE ENGLAND. TEL: 0181 943 5000 FAX: 0181 943 5850 **PRINTED IN ENGLAND BY:** BR HUBBARD PRINT, DRONFIELD, SHEFFIELD **COLOUR ORIGINATION BY**: ICON REPRODUCTION, LONDON SE1

THE AUTO TRADER RAC TOURING CAR CHAMPIONSHIP IS ORGANISED BY TOCA LTD, THE MANOR, HASELEY BUSINESS CENTRE, WARWICK CV35 7LS. TEL: 01203 537037 FAX: 01203 537038

Putting the spice back in the show

Alan Gow - TOCA Ltd

The *Auto Trader* RAC Touring Car Championship has come a long way since TOCA Limited took over the reins back in 1992. Today the BTCC is universally recognised as the most prestigious championship of its type in the world. We have increased the UK television coverage from around 200 minutes on the BBC in 1991 to more than 1000 in 1997 including, for the first time, live broadcasts. Over the same period, on-track crowds have grown from an annual total of 50,000 to in excess of 300,000 and the cumulative global television audience has spiralled from virtually nil to 1.2 billion viewers - a total which in racing terms is only topped by F1.

But, despite these mega-impressive figures, all is not rosy in the BTCC at the moment. To a large extent the series has been living on past glories - a hard earned reputation grown from close and exciting racing, coupled to more than the odd bit of panel bashing. Unfortunately the technological development of the machinery has seen the advent of the age old problem: today's cars are just too good - they handle and brake so well that drivers rarely get the chance to take advantage of the inadequacies of those in front. Sure, the racing is close but there needs to be more overtaking, more excitement and much more entertainment.

The technical regulations are stable for at least another three years, so it's up to the championship itself - in other words TOCA - to devise a way of putting the spice back into the show. The purists may cringe but the purists don't pay the bills. For the BTCC to remain at the top of international motorsport and also to encourage new audiences, we have to make it more watchable. At the same time, however, we do not want the BTCC to be anything other than a serious motorsport series. The best cars and the best drivers always deserve to win races, but we need to recreate the tension of 'will he or won't he?' rather than 'how much will he win by?'.

For 1998, TOCA is revising the format of the races to bring back the tension and anticipation; it's not a new idea, after all most top sports like cricket, football and rugby have changed their rules to improve both the live and televised spectacle.

Enjoy this book, enjoy the winter break and rest assured next year's *Auto Trader* Championship will be one to savour.

Action aplenty

David Owen-Smith - Auto Trader

Auto Trader and the RAC Touring Car Championship celebrated their fifth year of association in 1997. A continuing partnership in the world's greatest touring car series.

The series produced another fabulous spectacle for race fans, either attending the circuits themselves, or through the excellent television coverage that has brought touring car action to an even larger audience.

Our congratulations go to Alain Menu and the Williams Renault Dealer Racing team for their almost steamroller-like success in this year's championship. In their wake, the championship lived up to the crowd's expectations with good close racing and the inevitable action which makes touring car racing so exciting.

Auto Trader would like to thank all the spectators and race fans for their continued support and of course the teams, the drivers and all the people behind the scenes who make the event happen.

The 1998 *Auto Trader* Touring Car Championship starts in April. Be there.

Battle for Independents

Andy Knox - TOTAL Oil

Offering a quarter-of-a-million pounds – the biggest awards and prize fund in British motorsport – the 1997 Total Cup was a cliff-hanger. Four different drivers scored race wins in the Independents' division, and three of them lined-up for the last race of the season with a chance of winning the title.

In the end, 1990 BTCC Champion Robb Gravett (Rock-It Cargo Honda Accord) took the top step on the podium and the £75,000 cheque. Robb admitted he'd driven with his head rather than his heart, but that's often how titles are won.

Defending Total Cup champion Lee Brookes (Brookes Motorsport Peugeot 406) again scored more race wins than any of his rivals, but couldn't quite recover the ground lost through early-season mechanical failures. A year after winning the title and the big money, he was runner-up – and only just!

Colin Gallie equalled Brookes' points tally, but with less race wins he slipped to third on the tie-break. Although a Touring Car newcomer, Gallie (Team DCRS BMW 320i) led the Total Cup for most of the season, itself a fine achievement – and a reminder, as James Thompson will confirm, that the Independents' division can be a high-profile showplace for young talent.

VOLVO

THE NEW V40 T4

LUMBAR SUPPORT FOR YOUR BACK.
HEAD REST FOR YOUR NECK.
TURBO FOR YOUR ADRENAL GLAND.

The new Volvo V40 T4 is a car that will both confirm your expectations and confound them. Naturally, it comes laden with safety features, like the Side Impact Protection System, driver's and side airbags and ABS brakes. The seats, needless to say, are ergonomically designed. And when you fold them flat you get fifty cubic feet of space in the back. So far, so Volvo. Yet the T4 also has a 200bhp turbocharged engine, capable of 30-70mph in just 5.9 seconds† (The kind of acceleration that will take you effortlessly past the lengthiest of long vehicles.) So, to the warm glow of satisfaction that comes from owning a Volvo, you can now add the cold tingle of anticipation. The Volvo V40. From £16,130 to £24,630. Or from £344 per month via Volvo Contract Hire.

VOLVO. A CAR YOU CAN BELIEVE IN.

Le Champion

No longer the bridesmaid, Alain Menu achieved his dream by clinching the British Touring Car Championship title in dominant style. The Swiss ace proved the master on the track in 1997 and, as Jonathan Noble discovers, in doing so revealed a new side to his 'Nice Guy Come Good' character

Alain Menu sat in the Williams-Renault awning, playing and joking with his two children and chatting serenely with his wife, Caroline. It was typical of any happy, close-knit family except, in just 10 minutes time, the loving husband and caring father would be out on the track, pushing his Laguna to its limits and taking no prisoners with his rivals.

This contrast of the quiet family man and the single-minded ruthless racing driver very much sums up Menu. His charge to this year's *Auto Trader* RAC Touring Car Championship title was without compromise, highlighted by a move past team-mate Jason Plato at Silverstone that denied the Oxford-driver runner-up spot in the title chase,

while away from the track, Menu remained as...Swiss as ever.

'Nothing has really changed for me this year after winning the title,' explains Menu. 'I discussed winning the championship with Caroline when I could see it coming and I remember telling her not to be surprised if I cried when I won it. But I didn't feel at all like that when it happened.

'It was not a question of everything being done and dusted, it was just that it was done and what is next. I guess that if you win the championship at the last race then the feeling must be different, but because I had weeks to get used to the idea that I was going to get it, when I finally got it, it was almost as if it was just going to be my year anyway.'

Menu dutifully helped add the manufacturers' and teams' championships to his own crown and, after that, attention shifted to seeing Plato finish runner-up in the title chase.

At Brands Hatch in September, Menu sacrificed a second position for his team-mate, but in the final round of the series at Silverstone, he overtook Plato for the lead in the day's first race and that meant, ultimately, Frank Biela would secure second place by just one point.

That was a major talking point, not only because of Plato's apparent discontent at the move ('It's sad, we might reflect and think, "Maybe it shouldn't have happened'"), but because it provided clear evidence of Menu's ruthlessness on the track and, perhaps,

showed that he did not want Plato to finish runner-up because it would make his own title success look even better.

'It is not like that at all,' counters Menu. 'I wasn't too concerned about who finished second, my aim was to win the championship. I race for the team and Williams pay my wages. So if they tell me to do anything for the team, then I do it. But at Silverstone, I don't think it was a big concern to Williams or to Renault that Jason finished second, because otherwise they would have said to me, 'Alain, now you must help Jason.'

'If Williams would have asked me I would have helped him. Even Jason never came to see me before the race to ask if I could help him. I am not saying I would have, but he never came. To me,

Clockwise from left: Alain Menu was delighted when he clinched the title at Snetterton, but he was not as emotional as he thought he would be. Plato beats Menu at Silverstone, but it was too late to stop Biela finishing as runner-up. Menu did not have things entirely his way in 1997, here Plato leads the field at Oulton Park. Menu, Williams and Renault proved to be the dominant package of '97 though

it was not a problem.'

Menu himself is the first to admit that he had reservations about Plato when the team signed him. For the team leader, Plato's outward self-confidence and wicked sense of humour could have proved a recipe for disaster but, despite being outpaced in qualifying for the opening round of the series at Donington Park, Menu was rarely troubled by Plato, even if the pair were not exactly best friends.

'I always knew since the first test we did together that he is quick and he was going to be quick, so when he got the first two poles at Donington Park, I was not surprised. I am not saying I was not cheesed off, because obviously I was because I would rather be on pole

Clockwise from left: Menu the winner. Menu the team-mate. Menu the loving husband. Menu the caring dad

position than anybody else, but I was quite surprised.

'After that, his season was a bit up and down, and that is another point about Silverstone. When people say he missed the runner-up spot by one point and it was my fault at Silverstone, that is bollocks. The championship is not just one race, it is 24 races, and he lost the championship by himself.

'With the car we had, he should have finished second place in the championship, no problem, so I don't feel responsible for anything. Other than that, our relationship was very good and, if he had anything to ask, he knew he could come and I would tell him the truth. I said before the season started I was going to be a nice guy and that is what happened.'

'Nice guy' are two words that often crop-up when people talk about Menu the man. But Menu the racing driver has certainly drawn his fair share of criticisms for collisions and controversial moves since he joined the BTCC fray back in 1992. The man himself makes no excuses.

'For sure I am ruthless, because I don't give much room and I don't expect much room to be given to me. That is

motor racing, but saying that I think I am a clean racer and obviously in touring cars it is so close that shit happens. You've got to fight for positions and, if you don't fight, then there is no reason for Williams to employ you. I am out there to win.'

That competitive spirit carries over to his life away from the race-track. He does not play any sport, but still demands perfection in everything he does, be it in his preparation for a race weekend or just relaxing at home.

'Yes, I am very competitive, you should ask my wife. I was really bad when I was a kid, because I threw tantrums when I lost at games. I don't like losing. I am not sure that I like winning so much, it's just that in particular, if it is something that I am really interested in, I don't like losing.

He adds: 'People think I am laidback, but I can be a pain in the bum, to be honest, because I like to do my own thing. I am fairly selfish. I do what I want to do first and then there is Caroline and the kids.

'When I say I like to play with the kids, I don't play with them 24 hours a day, no way. If I read the paper, then I like to finish reading the paper, whereas

Caroline would stop doing what she does and go and play with them.'

His family means a lot to Menu and he has few qualms, if any, about them coming to every race. They provide a sanctuary from the goings on out on the track and are almost a home-from-home for him in the Williams awning.

'To be honest, it is mainly Caroline who wants to come as she is keen to be at race meetings and we bring the kids with us.

'Now, there is no problem, but when the kids were younger it would happen once a year that I would tell Caroline they could not come anymore, because one of the kids would cry in the middle of the night before the race and that would upset me.

'That does not happen anymore and it is good to have them along because I can relax and, after I have done my bit on the track, it is nice to play with them, so I can forget about motor racing. And in a way, if you don't think about racing all the time, it is easier to be focused when you go back.'

Motor racing remains very much Menu's life, however. He will start the 1998 BTCC season as favourite to retain his crown and, in the short-term future, he is happy to remain a driver.

But longer-term, he has begun to think about forging a new path in his career. 'I've never felt I had anything to prove in my career. I know I am good enough to drive anything, including Formula 1, and I am sure I could have done a good job in Formula 1, although there are another 30 or 40 guys like me.

'Now I am in touring cars, in a very competitive championship, and I count myself lucky to have one of the best seats available. I am happy with the job I do and long may it continue.

'Obviously I have got Menu Motorsport in Formula Renault and Spiders, but I can't see myself doing it for much longer because there is hardly any profit to be made, so what is the point? Having a successful touring car team, though, yes, I am sure I would be interested in that...'

Other drivers beware: Alain Menu has certainly not finished winning in the BTCC just yet.

Powering ahead.

Auto Trader is again the prime sponsor of the RAC Touring Car Championship. Published in 13 regional editions each packed with pictures of thousands of cars, there's no better way of bringing buyers and sellers together.

That's why Britain's best selling motoring magazine attracts nearly 2 million readers every week.

Auto Trader

Britain's favourite motoring weekly.

Stripped down Laguna

The cars Alain Menu and friends drive on a Sunday afternoon share only body shell and a few design principles with those in the car park at the local multiplex cinema and bowling alley.

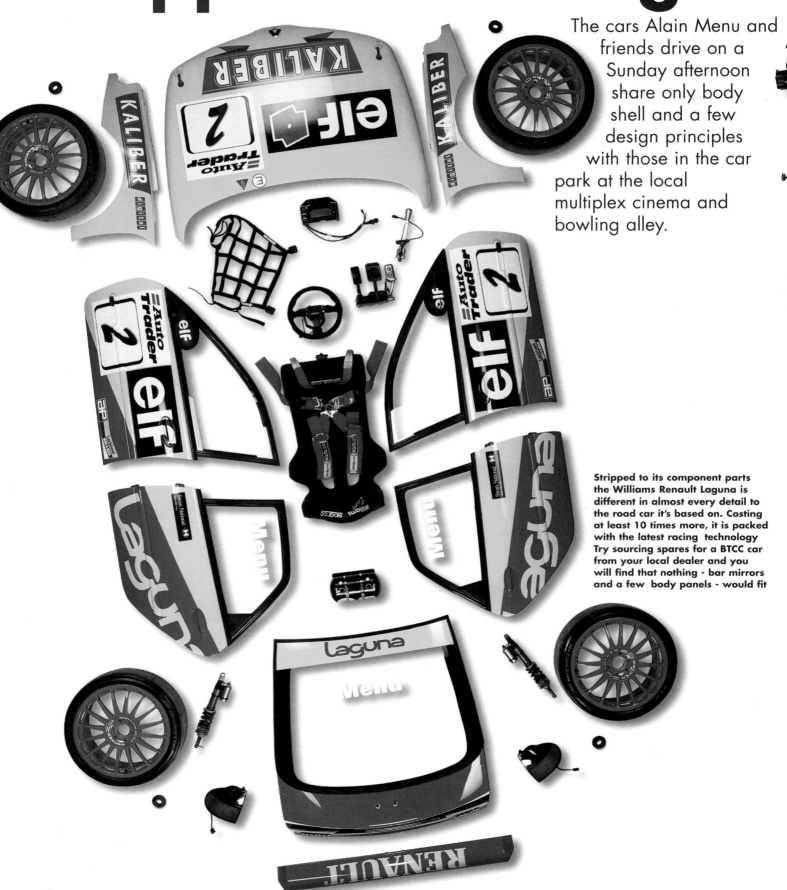

Stripped to its component parts the Williams Renault Laguna is different in almost every detail to the road car it's based on. Costing at least 10 times more, it is packed with the latest racing technology Try sourcing spares for a BTCC car from your local dealer and you will find that nothing - bar mirrors and a few body panels - would fit

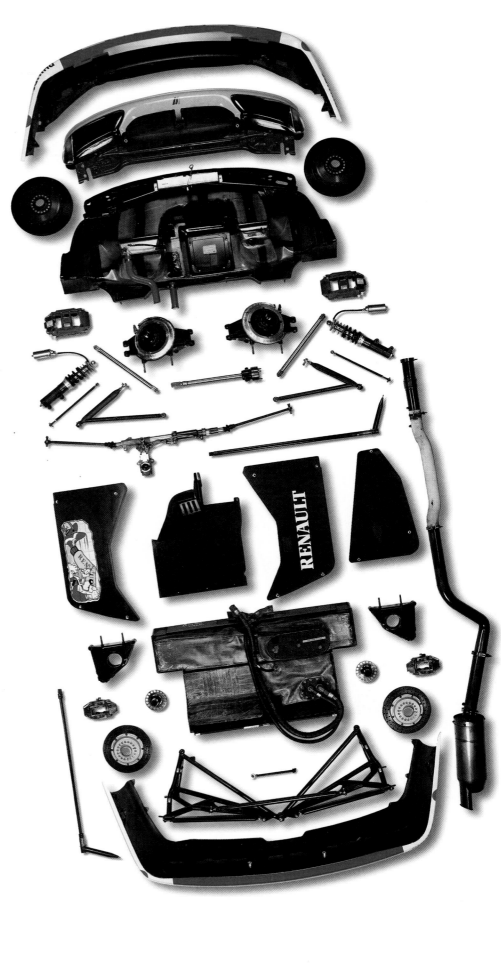

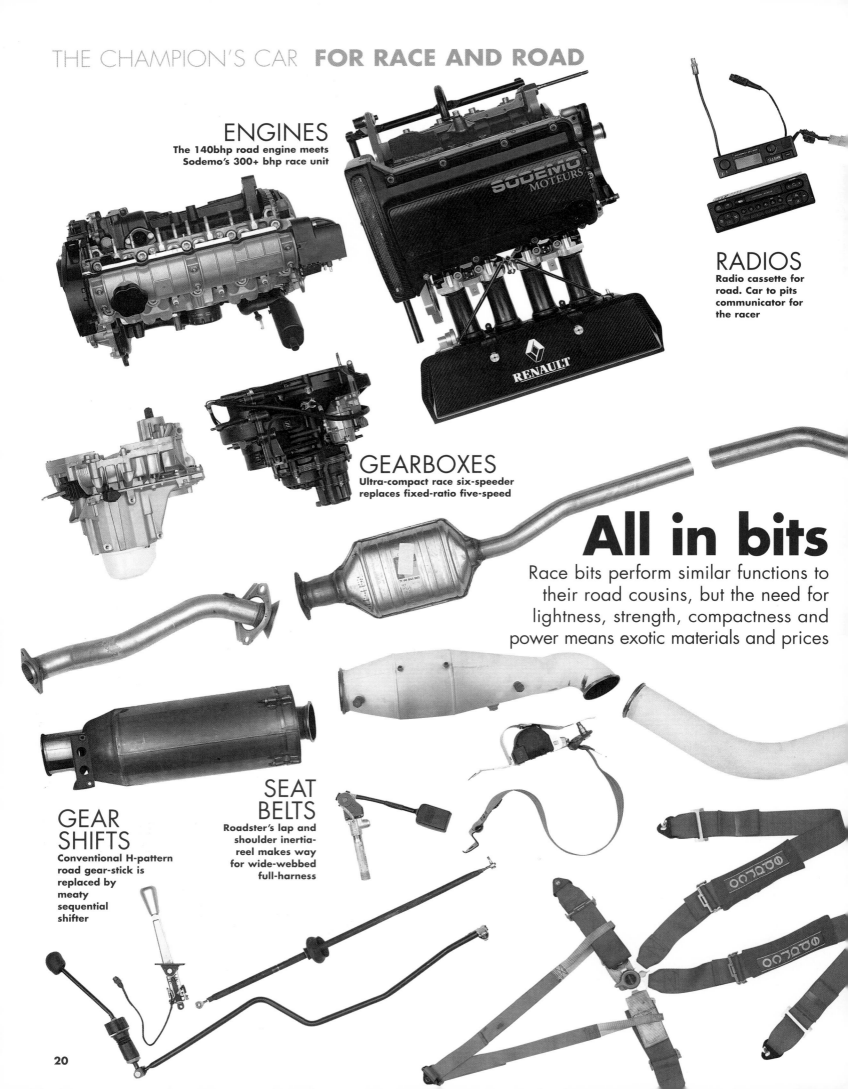

ENGINES
The 140bhp road engine meets Sodemo's 300+ bhp race unit

SODEMO MOTEURS

RENAULT

RADIOS
Radio cassette for road. Car to pits communicator for the racer

GEARBOXES
Ultra-compact race six-speeder replaces fixed-ratio five-speed

All in bits

Race bits perform similar functions to their road cousins, but the need for lightness, strength, compactness and power means exotic materials and prices

GEAR SHIFTS
Conventional H-pattern road gear-stick is replaced by meaty sequential shifter

SEAT BELTS
Roadster's lap and shoulder inertia-reel makes way for wide-webbed full-harness

SEATS

The road car gets a comfy, supportive perch, but safety requirements make the ultra-light race chair, with 'ears' to restrain the head in side-impacts, a very special bit of kit

STEERING WHEELS

Smaller race wheel loses airbag, gains radio buttons and engine kill-switch

EXHAUSTS

Bigger bore race pipe gives better gas-flow and power, but more noise. Both pipes have catalytic converters

TYRES

Nine-inch slick and grooved race Michelins deliver massive grip levels

CALIPERS

The race car's water-cooled multi-piston calipers deliver immense stopping power

BRAKE DISCS

Racer's 378mm (14.9 inch) ventilated front disc would not fit in Laguna road wheel (15-inch)

WHEELS

19-inch forged aluminium race wheels come in at around £1000 a throw

Who is king?

The BTCC is widely regarded as the best Super Touring championship in the world. With two ex-Grand Prix drivers among the cream of an incredibly strong crop of racers in '97, we asked BBC commentators Charlie Cox and Murray Walker to name their own personal top tens

Left: The line-up seen in 1997 was arguably the strongest in BTCC history. Alain Menu won the championship on the track, but was he regarded as the best driver out there? Right: Cox's and Walker's numbers are up

CHARLIE **COX**

Charlie Cox raced a private car in the BTCC as recently as 1995, but now commentates

1 ALAIN MENU
He is to touring car racing what Torvill and Dean were to figure skating. It was just perfect score after perfect score.

2 FRANK BIELA
He's the only man who actually looked smoother in his car than Alain Menu.

I think it is a big jump from the first two to third...which could be any one of four drivers.

3 JASON PLATO
Stunningly fast, but always seemed to be coming up from the back of the field and having to work his way through. Consistency will see him a champion.

4 JAMES THOMPSON
Flashes of incredible speed were yet again the hallmark of James Thompson, but this year he started to drive with his head. He grew into the role with Honda.

5 RICKARD RYDELL
An average season by his standards, he did his best with the car he had. Inexplicably not fully on the pace, but still consistent enough for fourth in the championship.

6 JOHN BINTCLIFFE
Anyone that can beat Frank Biela in the same machinery can't be omitted from this list. He may have had his critics in the past, but not any more.

7 ANTHONY REID
Controversial and clever, Anthony is one of the good old hard chargers and had come to terms with BTCC etiquette by the end of the year.

8 GABRIELE TARQUINI
A season of uncharacteristic mistakes mitigated by some strong finishes. He still has it in him to win many championships.

9 PAUL RADISICH
Another season of grace under pressure for the Kiwi, as the Ford showed improvement by the end of the year.

10 TIM HARVEY
He'll win the championship next year if it rains at every event!

James
10
OMPSON

Frank
1
BIELA

Jason
22
PLATO

Tim
12
HARVEY

MURRAY **WALKER**

**Murray Walker
is the voice of
both Formula 1
and the British
Touring Car
Championship**

1 ALAIN MENU
His record speaks for itself – three runner-up spots in the championship, followed by the BTCC title. Now he is where he deserves to be.

2 JASON PLATO
A truly outstanding debut year in the BTCC, he blew off everybody except his team-mate Alain Menu and multiple champion Frank Biela.

3 JOHN BINTCLIFFE
I've been ever more impressed with Bintcliffe's spirit and his ability. He mastered the Audi quattro and fairly won two races in his second season.

4 FRANK BIELA
He needs no words from me. This man is simply the best and proved it, despite the obvious weight penalty in his Audi.

5 RICKARD RYDELL
An outstanding driver and a nice person, sadly 1997 was a difficult year in a new car.

6 ANTHONY REID
I am enormously impressed with his spirit and aggression. He always gave us something to talk about.

7 JAMES THOMPSON
Like Rydell, I would have liked to put James higher, but for whatever reason the Honda and race circumstances did not enable him to shine often enough.

8 GABRIELE TARQUINI
A mysteriously disappointing year in which I had expected him to finish runner-up. In view of his past achievements and a mighty fine car, like James, I would have expected him to challenge at the front.

9 MATT NEAL
After struggling valiantly with the Mondeo, things at last came right with the Primera. Matt deserves a works drive, but will he get it?

10 DEREK WARWICK
Nice to see you back Derek! If he had had the right aerodynamic package he would really have flown. As it is, he certainly made John Cleland sit up and take notice.

23

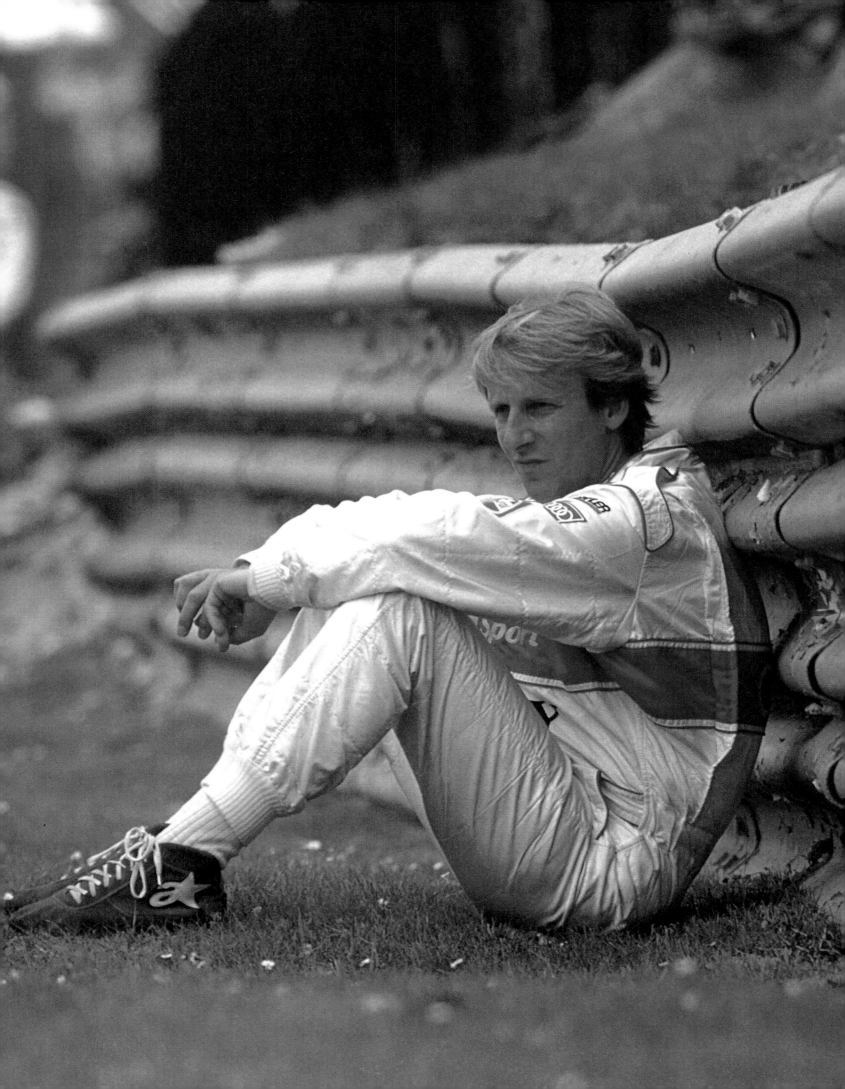

Thanks for the memories, Frank

Frank Biela said goodbye to the BTCC at the end of the year after two seasons full of victories, drama and good memories. The former champion reminisces with Nick Phillips

With 13 wins in two years, a championship win and a runner-up slot, Frank Biela has one of the best records in the history of the British Touring Car Championship. He rocketed onto the scene with a straight hat-trick of wins at the start of 1996 and has been a major player in the championship ever since. But now he's off again – back to race in his native Germany and taking with him lots of memories and opinions.

For Biela the best memories unsurprisingly come from early 1996, when he swept all before him. 'A very important race was the first one actually,' he says, 'because I had the impression that everybody thought "even if the Audis are competitive and successful in Germany and in Europe, they are probably not competitive in the UK." And then, in the very first race, we were competitive and we won both races – so I think that was one very important step, because before that race we really didn't know where we were.'

It got even better too and the third meeting of the year at Thruxton also rates very highly on the Biela feel-good scale. 'The win was very good,' he remembers, 'and,' he continues, referring to the extra 30kg penalty which followed shortly afterwards, 'maybe from a different point-of-view it was too good. But the more exciting and most important thing was the second race when I finished third after the crash in practice – coming from the back of the grid. I think that was a quite impressive event and I will never forget it.'

Biela sometimes looks so laidback when he's at the wheel that his speed comes as a surprise. Out of the car his attitude appears similar, but ask him questions and it's clear that, as in the car, he is constantly assessing and making his own judgements.

Overall Britain and the BTCC get a big thumbs up from Frank, with the possible exception of the food. 'Oh it's not that bad,' he says politely, 'but it's a different country, so you have to get used to it. Probably if you go to Europe you wouldn't like our food, but for us it is the other way round.'

He even professes to having enjoyed his time off-track: 'Yeah, definitely. I think last year was very exciting. It was quite interesting because I have been in the UK before, but only for a few days at a time in the past, so last year was the first time that I had a chance to look

For sale: Audi A4 quattro. One careful owner. Full service history. Good runner. Genuine reason for sale. **£275,000** o.n.o.

Choice of two.

Biela's assessment of the UK scene generally is a favourable one though: 'I think it's, let's say, one of the most competitive championships. I guess that Germany is quite equal. But I think if you look at the competitive teams, maybe we have a few more competitive teams in the UK, and probably we have some more competitive cars over here, even if the quantity is not that big.'

However, Frank's immediate future is back in Germany and he says the decision to go back was not too hard to take. 'Not really,' he says. 'The problem is that I'm really not sure if it will be so exciting over there, but I'm sure it is more important for myself because of television and the championship is now very well-known over there.

'When I came over here, we still had the ITC and I always had the impression that as a 2-litre car driver you were only second class. ITC is not there now and Super Touring is more important, so that is why I have to go back. The good thing is that in the last two years when I was in the UK they decided to race on some new circuits, so there are a few circuits which I don't know and maybe that's a bit better and makes it a bit more interesting. The new car and front-wheel drive will be a big challenge too and will keep my motivation up.'

Frank has certainly not closed the door on Britain forever and has frequently said that he would like to return in the future. 'I guess that I will be able to drive a racing car for another 10 years or something, so why not. As long as the championship is very good over here; as long as it is competitive and they have television coverage, and I think they are on the right track at the moment, I think there is the chance to come back, sure.'

An enthusiastic welcome, from both insiders and fans, awaits Frank if and when that opportunity arises.

around and play golf and everything and that was quite exciting. This year, I have tried to go home as much as possible.'

Certainly though there are aspects of the BTCC which he will miss greatly. The tracks, for example, are much more of a challenge than those he will return to in Germany. 'When I think about Hockenheim and the Nurburgring,' he says, 'I am really disappointed already.'

Ask him about the best British tracks though and he's much more enthusiastic, immediately naming the Brands Hatch Grand Prix circuit and Oulton Park as favourites, before turning the question round: 'I think we should do it the other way round – the most boring circuits.

'The most boring to me are Snetterton and Silverstone. All the others are exciting. The old circuits are bumpy and have funny lines, whereas in Germany or on most modern Grand Prix circuits, like Silverstone, it's quite normal – you enter the corner from the outside, go for the apex and come out at the exit. But at Oulton Park, you have tricky corners where the line is quite unusual and it's the same for Brands Hatch – that's why I like these circuits.'

The atmosphere among the drivers is also something he finds different to that in Germany and a big bonus. 'They always say that they have a good atmosphere in Germany, but to me it's not really true. I mean they talk to each other, but in the end they turn around and say something different. That's my opinion.

'But in the UK, it's very fair. Everybody knows, and they say it, that they have to beat this guy or this car or this team and that's it, but after the race you can do something together. Like

with Rickard Rydell last year, we were really fighting hard at Knockhill. I was going for a championship and he was trying very hard to push me off and things like this and, after the race, we went and played golf together and I think that's quite good. You know where you are and you know what the other people think about you.'

Apart from their sociability, Frank appreciates the driving talents of the Brit pack, not least team-mate John Bintcliffe: 'I've had to fight hard to beat him,' says Frank. 'Last year probably he had two or three good races. This year, especially in the second half of the season, he did a very good job all the time. He definitely is a very good driver and a tough competitor.

'If you look at Jason Plato, it's a similar situation. I mean I don't know what he did before, but I think it's impressive how he handled all the pressure. Although he was in the best team, he made the best out of it.

'There are a lot of good drivers in the BTCC. John and Jason are newcomers who did a very, very good job, and then there are the normal top drivers, people like Gabriele Tarquini, James Thompson, Rydell and Kelvin Burt.

'I was a little surprised about Burt that he was not that good, especially at the beginning I had the impression that he could really do a bit more than he did. Who else? Anthony Reid and David Leslie are good drivers, no doubt.

'Vauxhall, now there's a big question mark. I don't know how we should judge these drivers, but I'm sure they are, shall we say, not as bad as it seems. There are definitely quite a few very good drivers.'

Above: Frank Biela won 13 BTCC races in two seasons – not a bad record. Below: As the British fans will always remember him, on the limit in Audi's beautiful A4 quattro

Turn on, tune in, watch it

The BTCC took a big gamble with
the decision to go live on the BBC,
but, as Jonathan Noble explains,
it was a necessary move to ensure
the series' continued growth

Big brother was watching. Less than 24 hours after the broadcast of Chelsea's 2-0 demolition of Middlesbrough at Wembley in the FA Cup, arguably *the* biggest sporting event on the country's calendar, the British Touring Car Championship had its own day of days on the box.

At Brands Hatch, the ever-popular series went live to its mass audience for the first time. And, if the races themselves were not as exciting as the organisers, BBC officials or manufacturers' marketing men would have liked, it was at least a step in the right direction for the championship.

There had been much comment over the winter about whether TOCA's decision to broadcast three races (Brands Hatch, Donington Park and Knockhill) live was the right move. Opinions were split. Some saying that going live was the only way to confirm the BTCC's status as a mainstream sport, while others claimed that the often far from exciting racing would detract from the spectacle of those half-hour highlight packages that filled Saturday *Grandstand*.

'The simple reason is that the time is absolutely right for the championship to achieve a more dynamic profile, and establishing itself as a live television sport as well as an outstanding post-produced package is essential in that respect,' was *Grandstand* anchorman Steve Rider's argument in the build-up to the event.

And there was certainly no effort spared to achieve that goal. The statistics have been recounted time and again – the 25 cameras, the two helicopters to handle the microwave signals from the in-car cameras, the 14 miles of cable and the 60 technicians – but there were plenty of other logistical things that were not thought about.

At Brands Hatch for the first live broadcast, the technicians had to arrive on the Monday before the race to start putting their cables in. Work continued during the week but it was a bit sporadic – as it could only continue during breaks in the TOCA testing...

Live television also allowed the BBC to experiment with a bit of innovation that had not been seen before – but was soon to be afterwards – in the coverage of Formula 1. Take the split screen that was used to great effect and then later appeared on ITV, or even the live audio links with the drivers.

Although teething problems curtailed the latter's use at Brands Hatch, by Donington Park and Knockhill they were up and running – although a quick glance at the lap times of 'wired-up' John Cleland at Knockhill suggested that whenever he talked to Murray Walker his lap times suffered.

But despite the success of this season's broadcasts, that were executed relatively trouble-free, the series has to accept that it may not always be that way. The British weather, which rained off qualifying at Croft in June, could well play its part, as Nic Cristadoulou, the BBC logistics man, explained.

'In the past, bad weather has killed live events like the Boat Race and the (London) marathon,' he says. 'So we all tend to believe that the weather is God.

'And if you compare it with a football or cricket match, a live motorsport programme is much more of a challenge. For a cricket match, you only need seven cameras because the action is confined. But in motor racing, you have a much greater area to cover and miles of cabling which has all kinds of public and staff safety implications.'

There were a few losers from the live broadcasts as well. The Total Cup for Independents has always gained its fair share of coverage on the *Grandstand* highlights package, but on live television it barely got a foot in the door.

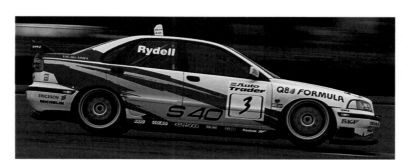

The general consensus after the three live broadcasts, however, is that the move has been a resounding success. The organisers seem happy, the manufacturers seem happy and, best of all, the public themselves seem happy.

Viewing figures from the live Donington Park weekend, the only one that came on the same weekend as a Formula 1 race, show it to be the sixth most popular sporting event of that week. The Canadian Grand Prix was top, with 5.92 million viewers, followed by England's football clash with Brazil (4 million), Greg Rusedski's Stella Artois semi-final match with Goran Ivanisevic (3.2m), more Le Tournoi football (2.7m), Formula 1 qualifiying (2.3m) and then the BTCC (2.2m).

What those in the know take more interest in, however, is the percentage share of the audience watching at that time. While the Grand Prix, Le Tournoi and the Stella Artios all grabbed about 34% of the audience, Formula 1 qualifying and the BTCC both drew 23% – well ahead of cricket's Benson & Hedges semi-final (5%), test match cricket (9%), and the British Lions' rugby tour of South Africa (14%).

Next season it seems all the BBC could ask for is more exciting racing in its three proposed live races and a few more of those famous incidents that happened on occasion this season – like the Alain Menu/Anthony Reid spectacle after their Brands Hatch collision.

Live television has been a step in the right direction, but for the championship to challenge football, cricket and tennis on both the airwaves and the newspaper columns it is going to have to remember that at times it's not just a sport, it's also entertainment. It must always strive to be bigger, better, faster and more.

Above: Innovative use of on-board cameras has played a key role in increasing the spectacle of touring cars on the box. Right: The BBC spared no effort in ensuring the live broadcasts were as trouble-free as possible

Winning the publicity war

Manufacturers use the British Touring Car Championship to enhance and change their images and so sell more cars. But it is Volvo who has perhaps used the BTCC better than any other company. Bruce Jones investigates

Top: The S40 racing programme represents the latest phase in Volvo's use of motorsport as an image enhancer. Right: The first phase was with the media-friendly 850 estate

To spectators the world over, touring car racing is simply about door-to-door racing with the added attraction of being able to cheer on the racing version of the car they drive on the road. But to the manufacturers, it's also about being seen to beat their rivals and establishing an image to spearhead their marketing campaigns. Just ask Volvo, for the Swedish manufacturer has arguably used its involvement in the British Touring Car Championship to better effect than the others.

When Volvo entered the BTCC in 1994, it did so specifically to promote a brand that sorely lacked a sporting image. And that aim has been pursued with increasing vigour ever since.

Volvo's Steve Reynolds explains: 'We took the decision to go back into motorsport four years ago and chose the series that would give us the best global reach – the BTCC. Being one of the last remaining independent manufacturers, we don't have the funds to go racing on the scale of the Renaults, Audis and Vauxhalls of this world and enter every touring car championship with cars developed centrally. We knew from the outset that we'd have to concentrate on one series and if you look at Alan Gow's figures of a potential global television

audience of nearly one billion viewers for the BTCC, it speaks for itself.

'Unlike rival manufacturers, Volvo shares its involvement in the BTCC with its dealers worldwide, taking the championship into markets where the dealers and the customers may not have seen the races or read about them.

'But this doesn't matter, as the imagery is strong, and so is the reputation of the British motorsport scene. Volvo's programme in the BTCC gives us the imagery we need to promote our product range and give it a sporting flavour. Dealerships use the TV footage to get the message across.'

When possible, Volvo brings people to see the racing, with almost 1000 of their 3000 guests at BTCC rounds last season being flown in from 22 countries.

The prime time for using Volvo's racing programme as an image builder is at the launch of a new model and thus the S40 racer has been busy supporting the launch of the T4, the performance version of the S40.

Reynolds elaborates: 'This year we launched the T4, bringing press in from around the world to Sweden, where we had the race car and a number of T4s at the Mantorp Park circuit. We ran passenger rides for every journalist on

that launch for a period of three weeks, so we put a lot of people through the car, with Rickard Rydell, Kelvin Burt and Swedish champion Jan Nilsson sharing the driving duties.

'Rydell was busy again in October with the Japanese S40 launch, and he was videoed driving Volvo Japan's chief executive around Mantorp, and talking about the model range. He has since been to Japan to launch the S40 to the dealers, all of whom have livery kits to put on road cars to make them look like the racer. It really is a big thing for us.'

Changing Volvo's image has certainly been a great success since the return to motorsport, Reynolds is pleased to report. 'We've changed as a brand considerably quicker over the last four years than we could ever have hoped,' he says. 'When we launched the racing programme we had an 850 without the T5 variant, which we launched halfway through that first season. Then there was a natural progression through the next two years as we launched the T5R in the second year and then the 850R in the third year. And, as a percentage of total 850 sales, the performance variants continued to increase their share.'

Then came the S40. 'Ah yes, we built a curvy car for a change,' laughs

Reynolds, 'and this has moved us on yet again. In fact, the whole product range has changed enormously. Anyone visiting Volvo's stand at the London Motor Show saw a convertible, a coupe and a whole range of sporting derivatives.'

Yet, to some, the image of a Volvo is still that of the 850 estate. And it was racing these that proved one of Volvo's biggest masterstrokes. 'That was extremely successful, we couldn't have brought anything any better,' reports Reynolds. 'The gag of putting the driver up through the sunroof with a dog next to him in the pre-race driver parade was excellent - the images still live on.

'Murray Walker's immortal words: "They thought Volvo were joking, but they're not laughing now," summed it up. It was a superb year for us. We knew it was going to be a learning year and that we were never going to win a significant number of races, but we certainly made an impact off-track.

'Looking ahead, we're reviewing which Super Touring championship will give us the best global profile and the jury is still out on whether that will be the British or the German. But, wherever we chose to go racing in 1998, we will continue to use touring car racing as the focus of our promotion.'

Main picture: The field swarms out into the country at Thruxton. Above left: Anthony Reid signs at Brands. Below left: Kelvin Burt tries rallying at Knockhill

Menu steals the show

Before the first round, the 1997 BTCC had looked pretty open, but Menu, Williams and Renault soon changed that, and, for the rest, writes Marcus Simmons, it was about what might have been

So, this was to be the most open *Auto Trader* RAC Touring Car Championship for years. Rickard Rydell would surely be a force in the TWR organisation's svelte new Volvo S40, returnee Gabriele Tarquini would fly in the Honda Accord now built and run by former World Rally Champion team Prodrive, defending champ Frank Biela was surely kidding that his four-wheel-drive Audi A4 would be bog slow, and Alain Menu could have a chance of stealing in for his first title if the Williams Renault Laguna had at least a modicum of reliability.

Dream on! TWR struggled with handling problems and straight-line speed on the Volvo, Tarquini and his Honda regularly threw away at least one race between them at each meeting, Biela was right, and Menu scorched to the most convincing and dominant BTCC success ever.

Twelve wins, 11 pole positions (13 if you count the two 'won' at Croft) and 12 fastest laps from the 24 races contributed to a storming season by the brilliant and ever-charming Swiss. And as if that wasn't enough, he blitzed the Bathurst 1000 enduro in Australia prior to mechanical problems, and then sprinted home at the end of the season to lift the £25,000 RAC Tourist Trophy at Donington Park.

In an off-season which saw more behind the scenes changes in the BTCC paddock than ever before, Williams Touring Car Engineering sowed the seeds for its successful 1997 attack by keeping three-time runner-up Menu on board as number one driver of the Laguna, which was now entering its fourth season. Crucially, ace designer John Russell produced a tidied up version of the yellow machine, which would continue to be powered by engines built by French specialist Sodemo, formerly the *bete noire* of the project. And tyre company Michelin, which supplied all the works teams except Audi, provided an astonishingly good product from day one.

Even so Williams, as much as any team, had its disruption. Out went team director Ian Harrison, off to play a part in setting up Triple Eight Race Engineering to run the works Vauxhalls, team manager Dick Goodman also split from the organisation, and Menu's veteran team mate Will Hoy made way for a newcomer.

In to fill the Harrison/Goodman breach was Belgian Didier Debae, most recently a key part of the German Schubel Engineering team while, after much prevarication and attempts to sign Tarquini, Hoy's replacement ended up being reigning Renault Spider UK Cup Champion Jason Plato.

Instantly the team gelled. Plato flew to pole positions for the opening three rounds, all won by Menu, who was to make it four on the trot in his start-of-season run. Incredibly, he had taken seven wins, just one short of the modern-day record, by round 10. From then on, the title was a formality, and he clinched it on August 10 at Snetterton, just one day after his 34th birthday.

The man commonly believed to be the greatest pilot of front-wheel drive Super Tourers in the world was a far more rounded driver this year. There were less moments of brilliance to make you gasp, less of that intangible element of watching someone extract what you would never have expected from a car which, rather than negotiating Donington Park's Old Hairpin sideways at over 100mph, should be ferrying the family, with beach balls, to the seaside at considerably less velocity.

But that was because the car was better. With Sodemo really getting their backsides kicked last year, the French firm pulled out all the stops on engine development – and made the motors reliable to boot. Therefore, Menu enjoyed the luxury of a clockwork car on which he could work to find a set-up in testing, rather than having to animal an unsorted machine to an unrealistic qualifying time.

Menu's race judgment – frequently criticised by members of the BTCC old guard – improved, probably for the same reason. Risks were no longer necessary. Instead, he could plan a race and make a measured, clear cut move, like when he passed Rydell at Croft. Only at Knockhill, when he had race two run-ins with the Swede and James Thompson, did that facade crumble.

By contrast, Plato's racecraft was, on occasion, fairly unimpressive, but that shouldn't detract from a season during which he shot onto the scene as a worthy addition to the series.

Plato's early-season pace was probably a bit of a red herring, Menu admitting later in the year that he always takes a while to get into gear. It had the effect of piling the pressure on the newboy, who went into a mid-season slump, brought on by overdriving while trying to replicate those early results.

But, by the end of the year, the Englishman was genuinely a match for his team leader on pace, and it led to an explosive BTCC finale at Silverstone, where the two fought tooth-and-nail all day. Lack of team orders may have meant that Plato lost out to Biela in the fight for championship runner-up spot but, with excitement like that, we should be thankful to Williams for not issuing them.

Audi was another team to allow its number two to step out of the shade on his own merits, Biela's cohort John Bintcliffe laying to rest any doubts over his ultimate ability by taking two fine wins, at Knockhill and Thruxton.

But it was a difficult title-defending

Above: It was all-change in the Vauxhall set-up and the season proved a struggle for all. Far left: Volvo showed snatches of real speed, but the S40 was not a consistent challenger. Left: Peugeot's first season with MSD was a mixed one, but there were some signs of forward progress

season for the total-traction silver and red A4s, run by the crack Audi Sport UK operation in Buckingham. Biela and Bintcliffe started the season still carrying the additional 30kg weight penalty dished out by the FIA in the wake of their dominance all around the world in 1996. But, after four meetings, during which Biela fluked a win at Thruxton in tricky wet/dry (and four-wheel drive friendly) conditions, the extra luggage was removed, enabling the Audis to revert to the 65kg disadvantage they had given away to their front-wheel-drive rivals prior to the previous mid-summer.

But that wasn't the only problem. Audi was disappointed with the relative lack of development progress made by Dunlop over the winter which, to the tyre company's credit, it rectified, but only over the course of the season. As well as that, the cars often seemed to show wildly unpredictable form from one qualifying session to the next. Indeed, from May onwards, no other team's drivers shared qualifying spoils as evenly at each meeting.

Biela knew he wouldn't be a factor this year, so it's to his credit that he strung together five race wins,

comfortably better than anyone bar Menu and quite often enough to win the title – in any other year. The German's reputation stayed high in 1997, and on his return to his homeland in '98 he will star.

Bintcliffe showed that he is ready to step into the limelight with those superb wins, which both came under intense pressure from his team mate. Into the bargain, he was saddled with a 1996 car, while his team mate benefited from any developments going. There were a couple of big shunts, as well as a silly prang with Biela in the May Thruxton meeting which saw his popularity with Audi dive to its lowest trough, but the Yorkshireman cleaned up his act and sparkled for the rest of the year.

TWR and Volvo probably didn't deserve to take fourth in the final standings as far as overall competitiveness was concerned, but at least the S40 was reliable, and Rydell was inspirational. The Swede was right not to leap to too many conclusions when the car set some stunning winter test times, because the 1997 season turned into a struggle to re-discover that form.

The narrow-track machine, which

replaced the boxy 850, oversteered in fast corners and understeered out of the slow ones, and its drivers – Rydell twinned with Kelvin Burt again – often found straight-line speed unimpressive. It was the sort of car where, if everything fell together for a lap, it would be right up there. Problem was, that lap would come only once in the season. At Thruxton, where Rydell took pole, he reported that he was 7kph up on the exit of the critical Church Corner than he had ever been before.

The win came at Brands Hatch, where a canny decision by Rydell saw him throw away fourth place in race one in a bid to try for a high grid position for the second, for which the starting order was decided by race one fastest laps. He duly converted that into a good start, and then battled past Anthony Reid's Nissan to give the S40 its first success.

Elsewhere, particularly on the bumpy, acrobatic circuits like Scotland's Knockhill, Rydell was staggeringly aggressive with the car, willing it to extremes it had no wish to encounter.

For smooth-driving former Formula 3 champion Burt, the year was a

disaster. Depressed by having to play the number two role to Rydell, he veered from pre-season buoyancy to mid-season despair, bar a strong performance at Donington Park which saw his race lead cruelly snatched away by an arbitrary jumped-start stop-go penalty.

Fifth and sixth in the points was a poor performance by Prodrive Honda Accord men James Thompson and Tarquini. For the English youngster, who had carried the fight to John Cleland in the Vauxhall team for two seasons, it was vindication that he really is destined for the Super Touring top drawer. Even the likes of Menu were quietly impressed with his form this year, which hit its peak when he outdrove his team mate to win at Brands Hatch in round eight.

Tarquini, though, was a disappointment. Quick, yes, but badly lacking in consistency. With a car as good as he had at his disposal, one win – in tricky conditions at Thruxton – was a bad return from the Italian. Too often his strong showings would be interspersed with undistinguished runs in the midfield, like at Donington in March and at Snetterton.

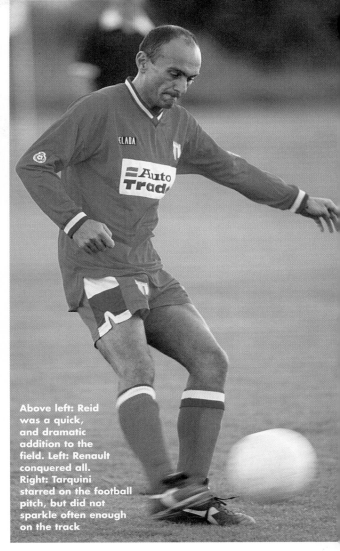

Above left: Reid was a quick, and dramatic addition to the field. Left: Renault conquered all. Right: Tarquini starred on the football pitch, but did not sparkle often enough on the track

Above: The Audis inevitably went well in the wet, but they also won more dry-track races than anyone but Renault. Below right: Ford turned in another learning year, and the Reynard/WSR Mondeos were showing promise by the end of the season

Rather than the Hondas, it was the Ray Mallock Limited Nissan Primeras which by the end of the year were providing the major threat to Renault. Veteran David Leslie comfortably took the lion's share of the points, having a decidedly sensible season as the car's form improved more and more. In the other machine, Anthony Reid provided the sparks, some sensational performances at Brands and Snetterton pock-marked with incidents and good old-fashioned bad luck.

Mallock did a good job with the Nissan. It nearly got on the podium at the first round, when it was less than a week old, and a front suspension tweak discovered mid-season was the final piece in the jigsaw of making a real contender. Reid ultimately took his and the new Primera's first win in a TT heat. There will be more next year.

The experience of the canny Tim Harvey allowed the 1992 BTCC champ to net an at-times unlikely top 10 spot for Peugeot in the final standings. Transferring the project from the company's UK headquarters to former Honda builder Motor Sport Developments was a step in the right

direction which could bear fruit in 1998, but '97 was a year of transition.

Flashes of form came at Thruxton and Donington, Harvey taking second at both tracks, but if anything he was being outdone by team mate Patrick Watts by the end of the season.

It was a typical Watts season. He tried hard, got into a few scrapes and didn't enjoy the best of fortune, but as a crowd-pleaser there are few to top him.

By the end of the season, genuine progress was being made with the Ford Mondeo built by Reynard and run by West Surrey Racing. The common sentiment is that Reynard, a winner first time out in Indycars, Formula 3000 and Formula 3, underestimated the BTCC,

and a severe steering problem caused some major early-season suspension geometry rethinks.

But Hoy and Paul Radisich gradually rose up the grids, thanks to hard work by the WSR engineers and the old pros behind the wheel. The Kiwi was nearly good for the podium by season's end.

Everyone at Vauxhall knew 1997 would be a difficult season, but it didn't start too badly for the brand new Triple Eight Race Engineering team. It got worse though. At first the 1996 Vectra was at least reliable, enabling Cleland and Derek Warwick comfortably into the points on a regular basis. But as others improved, and the Vauxhall boys continued to suffer because of the

inadequate aerodynamic kit developed by Opel in Germany, the cars became less and less competitive.

Cleland and Warwick both performed well, the ex-Grand Prix man in particular laying to rest any questioning of his Super Touring prowess in the wake of his bad year with Alfa Romeo in '95, but this was a season to endure.

Both Vauxhall's stalwarts are already talking a good race for the 1998 *Auto Trader* RAC Touring Car Championship. As are those at Honda, Nissan, Audi... And with Menu leading the Renault attack again, it could be the closest season for ages. Hang on, have we been here before?

37

Menu gets the perfect start

The experts had predicted that 1997 would be one of the most competitive seasons ever. But they had not counted on Alain Menu and Renault, who completely dominated at Donington Park.

Top: First corner action. Middle: Warwick had good reason to be pensive. Above: Pole man Plato. Right: Heavyweight Biela struggled

Renault domination was the name of the game as the BTCC season kicked off at Donington on Easter Monday. Alain Menu won both races and his new team-mate, Jason Plato, produced the season's first rabbit out of the hat with a pair of brilliant pole positions. In the tradition of previous champions BMW in 1993, Alfa Romeo in '94 and Audi in '96, the Regie had hit the ground running.

Before Easter it had all looked very open. There was no clear favourite and at least four contenders for the accolade, each with its strengths and apparent weaknesses. Audi would surely defend its titles vigorously, but was already

indicating that it felt the 30kg extra weight penalty it had picked up midway through 1996 would prove excessive.

Honda had the strongest engine and a base car with theoretical advantages, but would the switching of the programme from MSD to Prodrive cause problems?

Volvo looked very organised, as it had done for the past two seasons, but the S40, despite showing early potential, was still something of an unknown quantity.

Renault, meanwhile, had a settled team and a well-developed and very good chassis, but had suffered terrible engine reliability through 1996. Had the base engine, one of the oldest in the field, reached the limit of development?

Donington provided the first answers. The Renaults clearly had the edge on pace, though James Thompson's Honda was close enough in qualifying to keep them honest. Audi was not quite on the ultimate pace and Volvo provided the closest challenge in race trim.

With Plato unversed in the tricky business of making a decent Super Touring start and inexperienced at pacing himself to look after his tyres, it looked as though second fastest qualifier Menu was a good bet for the wins – and so it proved. Plato duly took second place in race one despite pressure from Rickard Rydell in the Volvo, who retired in the closing stages with team-

mate Kelvin Burt ultimately third.

The second race looked even easier for the Renault boys, until Plato's Laguna ground to a steamy halt as they were running one-two. The word was that a stone had punctured the radiator, leading to the failure, and it certainly boosted the morale of those hoping for Renault engine weaknesses.

Rydell this time was second and third-placed Frank Biela showed that, although the Audis did not look capable of winning, it could finish in the points.

Of the rest, Nissan looked to have the most potential with impressive qualifying speed and a fourth place for David Leslie in round one.

Above: It did not take long for the Williams to stake its claim as the car to have in 1997. Right: Alain Menu got the perfect start to his season

ROUND 1	18 LAPS	**ROUND 2**	18 LAPS
DRIVER	**CAR**	**DRIVER**	**CAR**
1 Alain MENU	Renault Laguna	Alain MENU	Renault Laguna
2 Jason PLATO	Renault Laguna	Rickard RYDELL	Volvo S40
3 Kelvin BURT	Volvo S40	Frank BIELA	Audi A4 quattro
4 David LESLIE	Nissan Primera	Gabriele TARQUINI	Honda Accord
5 John BINTCLIFFE	Audi A4 quattro	John BINTCLIFFE	Audi A4 quattro
6 Paul RADISICH	Ford Mondeo	James THOMPSON	Honda Accord
7 Gabriele TARQUINI	Honda Accord	Paul RADISICH	Ford Mondeo
8 Patrick WATTS	Peugeot 406	Derek WARWICK	Vauxhall Vectra
9 Derek WARWICK	Vauxhall Vectra	Kelvin BURT	Volvo S40
10 Tim HARVEY	Peugeot 406	Colin GALLIE	BMW 320i

Fastest lap Alain MENU   **Fastest lap** Alain MENU
Total Cup Colin GALLIE   **Total Cup** Colin GALLIE

Menu on course after fourth win

It may have been only the second round of the championship, but Alain Menu's double victory left him as the clear favourite for the title and his rivals wondering just how they could stop Williams Renault

Clockwise from left: Renault's fortunes were on the up as Audi's were deflating. No joy for Gabriele Tarquini or Honda. Anthony Reid's Nissan was left battered. James Thompson heads David Leslie across the start-finish line

A Clean Sweep.

MICHELIN

1997 BTCC Champions

Michelin Pilots continue their winning ways in the British Touring Car Championships, taking the 1997 driver, manufacturer and team titles with Alain Menu, Renault UK and Williams Renault Dealer Racing. This year's triumph brings the total number of Michelin wins in the BTCC to more than 70 since the world's number one tyre maker entered the fray in 1993. But the ultimate winner is you the motorist. Pilots tested to the limits in motorsport ensure you get tyres that excel on the road. Fit the sure winners to your car - Michelin Pilot high performance tyres.

MICHELIN *Pilot*

Two more wins for Alain Menu and the Renault Laguna at a bitterly cold Silverstone proved beyond doubt that the rest of the field would have to work much harder, although Rickard Rydell's pace in round three was impressive. Jason Plato's wonderful start to the season continued in qualifying, as he took his third straight pole, but with the first race the honeymoon came to an abrupt halt. Jason stalled his Laguna at the start and had to chase round after the field. He still scored well in race two with third place, but only after an appeal put him back in the results following initial exclusion for his part in a clash which put Kelvin Burt's Volvo out. Burt had provided some of the entertainment in the first race, when he made a great start to be second and then held team-mate Rickard Rydell up for several laps.

Once past, Rydell reeled Menu in and almost caught him in the final laps. It looked as though the S40 might be a match for the Laguna over a race distance – until the evidence from round four came in. Then Rydell had a much better shot at Menu, running second

from the early laps, but eventually finished much further back. The Swiss Renault driver looked so solid that already, after just two of the scheduled 12 meetings he was fielding questions about the inevitability of his championship victory. 'It's a fantastic start to the season,' he replied, 'but there are 20 races to go – it's not done yet.'

The most disappointed man in the field was James Thompson. He'd qualified alongside Menu on the front row for round four and genuinely reckoned he could beat him. However, an inter-race engine change left his Honda Accord leaking clutch fluid and, with the clutch dragging, he crept forward on the grid. He did lead the early laps, but the inevitable stop-go penalty for his jump-start was soon imposed and he was out of the equation.

At Nissan, there was more joy. David Leslie finished third to give the new Primera its first podium finish long before even the most optimistic team members had predicted, while at Audi it was all gloom with no score for John Bintcliffe and just one seventh place for Frank Biela.

Above: Burt holds off Rydell in race one as the Volvo teamsters hold their breath. Left: Watts heads Harvey as the Peugeot twins battle among themselves

ROUND 3	20 LAPS	**ROUND 4**	20 LAPS
DRIVER	**CAR**	**DRIVER**	**CAR**
1 Alain MENU	Renault Laguna	Alain MENU	Renault Laguna
2 Rickard RYDELL	Volvo S40	Rickard RYDELL	Volvo S40
3 David LESLIE	Nissan Primera	Jason PLATO	Renault Laguna
4 Kelvin BURT	Volvo S40	Tim HARVEY	Peugeot 406
5 Gabriele TARQUINI	Honda Accord	Derek WARWICK	Vauxhall Vectra
6 John CLELAND	Vauxhall Vectra	John CLELAND	Vauxhall Vectra
7 Frank BIELA	Audi A4 quattro	Will HOY	Ford Mondeo
8 Derek WARWICK	Vauxhall Vectra	Patrick WATTS	Peugeot 406
9 Patrick WATTS	Peugeot 406	James THOMPSON	Honda Accord
10 Jason PLATO	Renault Laguna	Robb GRAVETT	Honda Accord

Fastest lap Jason PLATO
Total Cup Robb GRAVETT

Fastest lap Alain MENU
Total Cup Robb GRAVETT

Biela ends Menu's run

Frank Biela's title defence was already off-course after Alain Menu's early season domination, but at Thruxton he got it right to score Audi's first win of the year

The rain came down at Thruxton and two new winners emerged to stop the Renault victory streak, but Alain Menu came out of the weekend an even stronger title favourite than he'd been before. The Swiss ace dominated qualifying in the dry to be on pole for both races, but with a series of showers making the circuit treacherously slippery – dangerously so, according to the weekend's highest scorer Gabriele Tarquini – Menu played the percentage game and settled for safe solid points for two third places.

The wins went to Frank Biela in the Audi and Tarquini's Honda. Biela used his four-wheel-drive to its best advantage at the start of round five to lead by the second corner. The big challenge came from Tarquini, who even led for a while in the Honda Accord after Biela had a big moment at the ultra-fast Church corner.

By the end though the Audi was ahead again, with Tarquini second and Menu a composed third. Biela's luck ran out in round six when a clash with team-mate John Bintcliffe on the first lap put him heavily into the barriers.

Tarquini led the field on a dry track, chased by team-mate James Thompson and Menu, but the safety car was scrambled while Biela's wrecked Audi was recovered and, as the field trudged round slowly behind it, the rain came down again. At the re-start Tarquini maintained his advantage, but Thompson came under pressure from Menu.

The Renault was soon second and looking for a way into the lead, before Menu again opted for long-term gain and eased off. Meanwhile, a group of cars had pitted to fit wet-weather rubber and these were scything through the pack, led by Tim Harvey's Peugeot 406.

By the end Harvey was second and with just one more lap, he would certainly have scored Peugeot's first BTCC win. However Tarquini held on for the victory with Menu third ahead of the second wet-shod car - Anthony Reid's Nissan Primera.

As is often the case when the weather throws an extra variable into the BTCC equation, it had been an entertaining day's racing with plenty of surprises and not a few disappointments. Chief among the disappointments was Volvo's form. Rickard Rydell drove a pair of excellent races, but the S40's qualifying pace was well off and the Swede left Hampshire with just a pair of fifth places and a big dent in his claim to be Menu's biggest title challenger.

ROUND 5	18 LAPS	ROUND 6	22 LAPS
DRIVER	**CAR**	**DRIVER**	**CAR**
1 Frank BIELA	Audi A4 quattro	Gabriele TARQUINI	Honda Accord
2 Gabriele TARQUINI	Honda Accord	Tim HARVEY	Peugeot 406
3 Alain MENU	Renault Laguna	Alain MENU	Renault Laguna
4 John BINTCLIFFE	Audi A4 quattro	Anthony REID	Nissan Primera
5 Rickard RYDELL	Volvo S40	Rickard RYDELL	Volvo S40
6 James THOMPSON	Honda Accord	Derek WARWICK	Vauxhall Vectra
7 David LESLIE	Nissan Primera	Jason PLATO	Renault Laguna
8 Anthony REID	Nissan Primera	John BINTCLIFFE	Audi A4 quattro
9 Tim HARVEY	Peugeot 406	John CLELAND	Vauxhall Vectra
10 Paul RADISICH	Ford Mondeo	Paul RADISICH	Ford Mondeo

Fastest lap James THOMPSON
Total Cup Matt NEAL

Fastest lap James THOMPSON
Total Cup Matt NEAL

Clockwise from above: Rain would be the talking point at Thruxton. Harvey proved his wet-weather mastery with a second place. Biela looked more relieved than happy after winning

Clockwise from top: Tarquini on his way to a well deserved victory. Tyre choice decisions would prove crucial. No joy for the Vauxhall twins. The BTCC is all about team-work

'Well it was like this...' Anthony Reid explains his dramatic day to Nissan people and Michelin men

Centre: The men from the Beeb did it live at Brands. Left: David Richards leads the Honda cheering team

Honda hits the pace at Brands

Alain Menu won again in round seven, but a couple of hours later he could do nothing about the Hondas of winner James Thompson and Gabriele Tarquini

Brands Hatch hosted the first BTCC rounds to be broadcast live on the BBC in the current era and, in a couple of races short on overtaking but long on close racing and controversy, Alain Menu again increased his advantage over the field.

Menu won the first of the two rounds in dominant style, but the second went to Honda's James Thompson with Menu seemingly unable to improve on third place before becoming embroiled in a heated on-track incident with Nissan's Anthony Reid which saw them both off the track and Menu fuming.

Round seven was business as usual, with Menu winning from pole position, chased by Thompson and Jason Plato in the second Renault. The Brands Hatch Indy circuit tends to act as a leveller, with cars very evenly matched on lap times. This is partly because it is so short and partly because it is a momentum track so that power and traction deficiencies are less obvious.

The only driver/car combination seemingly capable of consistently passing others here was Reid and the Nissan. The Scot had put himself in a position where he had to make plenty of moves when he made a couple of less than impressive starts. In race one he blew his getaway big time and dropped to 10th. That was good news for the crowd both at Brands and in front of their TVs, because he had battled his way up to

FINA

Above: Brookes buries his Peugeot in the Paddock gravel. Right: Watts follows suit

Left: Reid's Nissan and Menu's Renault head for trouble after clashing at Clearways

fifth place by the end.

For race two, the Hondas of Gabriele Tarquini and Thompson were on the front row and, after Thompson out-gunned his pole-sitting team-mate off the line, they settled into a calm and unruffled run to the chequered flag. Menu was third in the early laps, neatly placed to keep hauling in the points, but unable, as he admitted later, to mount a serious challenge to the Hondas.

The fun was again coming from Reid.

His start was a little better this time, as he dropped only from fourth on the grid to fifth. Rickard Rydell was ahead of him in the Volvo and Reid harassed him long and hard, before finally slipping past with a great move into Paddock. He quickly closed in on Menu and immediately tried his luck at Clearways. That's when it all went wrong as the Nissan locked up and slid into the back of the Renault, sending both off the track. Both returned to the fray, Menu

to fifth place behind David Leslie's Nissan and Plato, and Reid well down the field. Plato, following team orders, let Menu through before the flag to give the points leader fourth place.

The row continued later. 'He's a complete loony,' fumed Menu after the race. Reid apologised, but the stewards weren't impressed, fining him £1000. It was a sad end to the day, but it at least gave the men from the BBC a lifeline on a day which hadn't offered much else.

Left: Thompson discusses winning set-ups with the Prodrive engineers

All you need is Radio TOCA

Radio TOCA's second year saw the *Auto Trader* RAC Touring Car Championships's own broadcasting station produce an even better blend of music, race-chat and commentary.

Fronted by *Autosport's* John Hindhaugh, the mobile radio station, supported by both *Autosport* and sister magazine *Autocar*, was a permanent fixture in the touring car paddocks from Brands Hatch to Knockhill.

Operated by Bob Boote's ARB organisation, which has long looked after the public address needs of most UK race-tracks, Radio TOCA increased the range and quality of information reaching the fans.

Its FM transmitter spread the word over a radius of about 30 miles round each track. Starting the morning with music, chat and traffic information, the station moved into full-race mode during the course of the day, broadcasting the expert commentary of Robin Bradford, Ian Titchmarsh and their team to bring each race and qualifying session alive. Topical interviews, both with the stars of the feature BTCC races and some of the top-guns in the excellent package of support events, were blended into the commentary to provide the very best in spectator information, and entertainment.

Then, as the qualifying or race days wound down, Hindhaugh and the Radio TOCA crew were there again, doing their bit to keep homeward-bound racegoers informed about local traffic hold-ups, return to the issues and incidents of the day and sooth the nerves of any unlucky enough to be stuck in jams with a top selection of rock classics, current hits and kicking dance music.

	ROUND 7	38 LAPS	ROUND 8	38 LAPS
	DRIVER	**CAR**	**DRIVER**	**CAR**
1	Alain MENU	Renault Laguna	James THOMPSON	Honda Accord
2	James THOMPSON	Honda Accord	Gabriele TARQUINI	Honda Accord
3	Jason PLATO	Renault Laguna	David LESLIE	Nissan Primera
4	David LESLIE	Nissan Primera	Alain MENU	Renault Laguna
5	Anthony REID	Nissan Primera	Jason PLATO	Renault Laguna
6	Gabriele TARQUINI	Honda Accord	Frank BIELA	Audi A4 quattro
7	Rickard RYDELL	Volvo S40	Paul RADISICH	Ford Mondeo
8	Kelvin BURT	Volvo S40	Kelvin BURT	Volvo S40
9	Frank BIELA	Audi A4 quattro	John CLELAND	Vauxhall Vectra
10	Derek WARWICK	Vauxhall Vectra	Tim HARVEY	Peugeot 406

Fastest lap Alain MENU **Fastest lap** Alain MENU
Total Cup Robb GRAVETT **Total Cup** Robb GRAVETT

Menu flattens all opposition

Alain Menu was unstoppable on his favourite circuit, winning both races in a style which left the rest of the field reeling

Above: Harvey parked the Peugeot after the engine blew. **Right:** Meditation time for Reid, or is he checking suspension? **Middle right:** First corner mayhem. **Bottom right:** Tarquini runs for cover. **Far right:** Paul Radisich heads for Lodge

If the field reckoned they were getting a handle on the Menu problem at Brands Hatch, they were slapped back down again in hugely emphatic style in rounds nine and 10 at Oulton Park. Alain Menu quite simply was in another universe to the rest. Comfortably on pole for both races, he took another brilliant double win.

Menu's dominance made an even bigger impact on the points table than it might have, since Gabriele Tarquini, second before the weekend, failed to score and Menu's was the only name which featured in the top three for both races. The Swiss had to put in some serious work to win round nine. He'd fluffed his start and dropped to third place behind Jason Plato and Frank Biela, but this time there was no question of him settling for third place. Having quickly worked his way past Biela - outbraking him into Lodge, a move which he was justifiably proud of - he closed up on Plato and breezed past before pulling away to win.

Round 10 was much easier. Menu

Above: Plato leads Biela and winner Menu early in race one. Right: Menu and Plato celebrate. Above right: Cleland's Vauxhall Vectra was fifth in round nine

ROUND 9	30 LAPS	**ROUND 10**	27 LAPS
DRIVER	**CAR**	**DRIVER**	**CAR**
1 Alain MENU	Renault Laguna	Alain MENU	Renault Laguna
2 Jason PLATO	Renault Laguna	James THOMPSON	Honda Accord
3 Frank BIELA	Audi A4 quattro	Rickard RYDELL	Volvo S40
4 John BINTCLIFFE	Audi A4 quattro	Jason PLATO	Renault Laguna
5 John CLELAND	Vauxhall Vectra	John BINTCLIFFE	Audi A4 quattro
6 Rickard RYDELL	Volvo S40	David LESLIE	Nissan Primera
7 Anthony REID	Nissan Primera	Paul RADISICH	Ford Mondeo
8 Paul RADISICH	Ford Mondeo	Tim HARVEY	Peugeot 406
9 Kelvin BURT	Volvo S40	Lee BROOKES	Peugeot 406
10 David LESLIE	Nissan Primera	Colin GALLIE	BMW 320i

Fastest lap Alain MENU
Total Cup Colin GALLIE

Fastest lap Alain MENU
Total Cup Lee BROOKES

made a decent start and the rest were heavily delayed by the second of the day's two startline accidents. In the first, James Thompson had been put out of the running, while in the second any chance he might have felt he had to challenge Menu disappeared when he emerged from the fracas behind the fast-starting Audi of John Bintcliffe.

Thompson eventually made it past Bintcliffe, but by then Menu was long gone and the Honda was in no position to challenge. James still finished second though, ahead of Rickard Rydell in the Volvo. This was a great performance from the Swede who, courtesy of the shunt, had been down to 10th place on lap one. A similarly fine, though much wilder, drive came from the man who'd been second in race one, Plato. He too was delayed and had survived three off-track moments during his blast up to fourth from 17th.

Bintcliffe pushed his tyres too hard, but still finished fifth to complete an encouraging day for Audi on the weekend when the additional 30kg weight penalty that it had been running with since the middle of 1996 was removed. Bintcliffe had been fourth in round nine, behind team mate Biela.

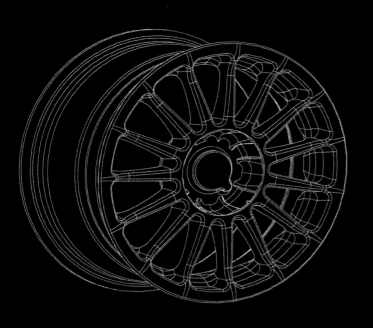

Precision

Perfection

Performance

Menu and Biela reign

Alain Menu again made the most of things as rain livened up proceedings for the BBC's second live broadcast. Renault's number one took victory in round 12 and Frank Biela won round 11

Right: Biela took advantage of the damp to win the first race. Below: The Audi team welcomes its winner

The second live TV meeting was also one of the most entertaining and, needless to say, it was that man Menu who had the best of it with a win and a second place. Rain, a chaotic mix-up behind the safety car and plenty of overtaking had nevertheless combined to produce top-class BTCC fun.

Round 11 started on a damp track and the Audi men took full advantage. From sixth and seventh places on the grid, Frank Biela and John Bintcliffe stormed into first and second places by the first corner, Redgate. Tim Harvey, in the on-form Peugeot 406, and Menu headed the chasing pack.

Menu soon disposed of Harvey to

take third place and, as the track started to dry, so he gradually closed in on the Audis. With just a couple of laps to go he nipped past Bintcliffe who had dropped away from leader Biela to concentrate on defence when Menu started to challenge. Biela though held on to win from Menu and Bintcliffe.

The real drama was reserved for round 12. Kelvin Burt in the Volvo S40 had come within an ace of beating Menu to pole and in the race he had a brief moment of glory at the front, before it all fell apart for the local man. From the lights, Menu went straight into the lead from Burt and Gabriele Tarquini, but then dropped behind his two closest

Clockwise from right: Rydell leads race one star Burt. The train rounds McLeans. The Vauxhall men cogitate. Harvey's second place in race one gave Peugeot a big boost. Thompson, Harvey and Plato battle

pursuers after the Laguna snapped into oversteer at McLeans.

Then came the news that, although they had not made up any places off the grid, both Burt and Tarquini had jumped the start and would have to come in for stop-go penalties. A further spanner was then chucked into the works by Independent Robb Gravett. He had crashed at Redgate and the safety car was scrambled. Burt dived into the pits immediately, but Tarquini stayed out for the one lap the safety car stayed out. That led to a big-time bust-up as the race got under way again.

Tarquini pursued the safety car into the pit lane and second-placed Menu, initially followed him - aware that he

should not pass until the start-finish line. With the rest of the pack hard on the throttle Donington soon started to resemble the fast lane of the M25 after another round of the Crass Commuter Concertina Cup. In the confusion, Menu got away clear, chased by Harvey, while the big losers were Plato, who sustained too much damage to continue, and Thompson who was spun out and was firmly last when he re-joined.

That was it for the race for the lead, with Menu cruising home ahead of Harvey, Biela and Bintcliffe, but there was still plenty of fun to be had, with a slow Rickard Rydell bottling up a stack of quick guys to provoke some of the best mid-field tangles of the season.

ROUND 11	25 LAPS	**ROUND 12**	26 LAPS
DRIVER	**CAR**	**DRIVER**	**CAR**
1 Frank BIELA	Audi A4 quattro	Alain MENU	Renault Laguna
2 Alain MENU	Renault Laguna	Tim HARVEY	Peugeot 406
3 John BINTCLIFFE	Audi A4 quattro	Frank BIELA	Audi A4 quattro
4 Jason PLATO	Renault Laguna	John BINTCLIFFE	Audi A4 quattro
5 Rickard RYDELL	Volvo S40	Patrick WATTS	Peugeot 406
6 James THOMPSON	Honda Accord	Gabriele TARQUINI	Honda Accord
7 Tim HARVEY	Peugeot 406	Rickard RYDELL	Volvo S40
8 Kelvin BURT	Volvo S40	John CLELAND	Vauxhall Vectra
9 David LESLIE	Nissan Primera	Will HOY	Ford Mondeo
10 Patrick WATTS	Peugeot 406	Derek WARWICK	Vauxhall Vectra

Fastest lap Alain MENU
Total Cup Lee BROOKES

Fastest lap Gabriele TARQUINI
Total Cup Lee BROOKES

Live TV needs top-class racing

This was the year when the BTCC took the big step of putting three meetings out live on the BBC.

The move was certainly a success, but although rounds 11 & 12 were action-packed the other two featured-meetings suffered from racing that was less than rivetting. The BTCC has benefited over recent years from BHP's skilful editing of race footage to come up with recorded programmes for the BBC to broadcast which frequently flattered the quality of the racing. When the race is going out naked and unprotected by BHP's magic and there is little real excitement, it shows.

The BBC's live coverage is first class and its commentators do their best to hype things up, but the only lasting answer to the problem is to improve the quality of the racing.

Throughout this year the Super Touring Technical rules have been under review, with one of the biggest subjects on the agenda the need to improve racing, but in the end the 14 manufacturers involved decided by a large majority to do very little to the rules and the international governing body, the FIA, endorsed that. That means the onus is now very firmly on series organisers like TOCA to put life back into the races through their sporting regulations. TOCA chief Alan Gow has promised a radically revised format for '98.

Options include revisions to tyre rules - either to specify a control tyre or to insist that tyre companies can supply exactly the same tyres to all their BTCC customers - or adjustments to qualifying rules. All these ideas and more will be considered by TOCA, the manufacturers and teams over the early part of the winter.

Whatever the outcome of the discussions, there is consensus among most of those close to the sport, if not all the manufacturers, that something must be done to spice up the sport. The BBC live meeting count stays at three for 1998 but to really develop its place as a major sport the BTCC needs to have most if not all its races broadcast live and that won't happen unless the racing starts to sizzle again.

Menu triumphs in Croft chaos

Nothing could stand in the way of Alain
Menu's BTCC title charge. As all
about him lost their heads on
the revised Croft circuit, the
Swiss ace drove to a
well desered double

Croft's debut on the BTCC calendar was fraught with problems. Rain, safety worries plus a host of bizarre shunts and off-track excursions made for a dramatic weekend in the north-east.

Torrential rain was the first hurdle for the enthusiastic Croft promoters. There was so much of it that the track was flooded on Saturday when qualifying should have taken place and with deep puddles on several parts of the track there was no question of cancelling the day's activities.

Once the weather had eased and a massive overnight pumping operation had cleared the track, the field lined up in championship order.

That, of course, suited Alain Menu who would be on pole again for both races. He did not, however, make the best of it in round 13, being beaten away by Rickard Rydell's Volvo. In the early laps Menu was quite happy to settle for second place, comfortably clear of Frank Biela's Audi, which had punted team mate John Bintcliffe's A4 off in the early running. But, when Gabriele Tarquini forged past the Audi and rapidly closed in on Menu, the championship leader decided that attack was the answer and went after Rydell. Before long Menu had taken the lead, but he was not safe yet as Tarquini had also demoted the Volvo. For once, Menu looked as though he might be beaten for speed, but then Tarquini fell off while lapping Robb Gravett's Accord and the fight was over.

Round 14 was full of drama. First lap biffs shuffled the order and brought the safety car out. When the race re-started, Menu led Bintcliffe, Biela, Plato and Thompson. Bintcliffe ran wide at Tower and was passed left and right on the way up to Sunny. There Plato ran into Biela, pitching the Audi into the mud. Suddenly Thompson was second, although nearly four seconds behind Menu. Over the next eight laps, Thompson niggled away and reduced the lead to less than a second. 'He was really quick,' said Menu later. 'It was a tricky one and it would have been interesting if it had run the full distance.'

But soon it was all over. First Tarquini lost it coming onto the back straight, hit the wall hard and bounced back into the track. Out came the safety car for three laps while the track was cleared and then halfway round the first lap of the re-start Thompson had an identical shunt. With Thompson very shaken, the race was stopped and the results were taken a lap back, so he kept his second place, with David Leslie third to notch up another podium finish for Nissan.

Above: Croft brought plenty of close racing once (left) the track had dried out

Left: Thompson was on form for Honda before his crash. Below: Team members rush to help him

Right: BTCC boss Alan Gow shelters from the storm. Middle: Rydell took a third

Above: Bintcliffe spins after a tap from team mate Biela. Left: Yes, it really was wet

ROUND 13	25 LAPS	**ROUND 14**	18 LAPS
DRIVER	**CAR**	**DRIVER**	**CAR**
1 Alain MENU	Renault Laguna	Alain MENU	Renault Laguna
2 Jason PLATO	Renault Laguna	James THOMPSON	Honda Accord
3 Rickard RYDELL	Volvo S40	David LESLIE	Nissan Primera
4 Frank BIELA	Audi A4 Quattro	Jason PLATO	Renault Laguna
5 James THOMPSON	Honda Accord	John CLELAND	Vauxhall Vectra
6 John CLELAND	Vauxhall Vectra	John BINTCLIFFE	Audi A4 Quattro
7 Derek WARWICK	Vauxhall Vectra	Tim HARVEY	Peugeot 406
8 Will HOY	Ford Mondeo	Rickard RYDELL	Volvo S40
9 John BINTCLIFFE	Audi A4 Quattro	Anthony REID	Nissan Primera
10 Tim HARVEY	Peugeot 406	Derek WARWICK	Vauxhall Vectra

Fastest lap Gabriele TARQUINI
Total Cup Matt NEAL

Fastest lap Alain MENU
Total Cup Robb GRAVETT

AND YOU THOUGHT A MEG

The sublime curves of the new Peugeot 406 Coupé are the work of none other than the celebrated Pininfarina design house. Once behind the chrome instrument panel, aluminium gearstick in hand, the beauty of a 3.0 litre V6 engine is also evident. As a counterpoint to its breathtaking acceleration, Brembo brakes are fitted on all V6 models. There's a

RIVE WAS A VIDEO GAME.

choice of 3.0 litre and 2.0 litre models, manual and automatic, available from £20,360 to £28,020.* For more

information, simply call 0345 555 406.* The Peugeot 406 Coupé. Looks like it's game over for the rest.

THE NEW PEUGEOT 406 COUPÉ. THE DRIVE OF YOUR LIFE.

Bintcliffe's first; Audi's weekend

John Bintcliffe came of age at Knockhill to claim his maiden BTCC win after a hard-fought duel with team-mate Frank Biela. Their positions would be reversed later as the Audi proved the thing to have

Knockhill is different. Narrow with big kerbs and plenty of gradient changes, it is also the one track the circus visited this year, for rounds 15 & 16, on which the Renault Laguna was in no position to fight for wins.

The whole weekend in Scotland indeed seemed to have come through a time-warp from early 1996. In short it was Audi domination time. The only real difference from early '96 was that John Bintcliffe, no longer a rookie, was out to prove that he could now match team leader Frank Biela all the way. And he did just that.

The two Audi drivers shared all the top prizes equally. Each took a pole position, a win and a second place. In qualifying for the first race Bintcliffe made the cannier tyre choice and snatched pole. That gave him all the advantage he needed in the race, and although Biela piled on the pressure, the Yorkshireman hung on to take a well-deserved first BTCC win. In the second race the positions were reversed with Biela on pole and leading all the way, despite pressure from Bintcliffe.

The other big story was that Alain Menu had shown fallibility. A strong third in round 15, unable to live with the Audis but still clear of the rest, he got involved in a series of traffic tangles in round 16, first with James Thompson and then Rickard Rydell, and eventually retired. It would be his only non-finish of the season.

Behind the Audis, the minnows had fought things out. In round 15, fourth-placed Rickard Rydell headed a tight group throughout. Anthony Reid led the challenge for Nissan, but despite his best efforts he could find no way past, although he still claimed the honour of top Scot. James Thompson and Gabriele Tarquini had shadowed Reid all the way, waiting for an error that never came.

In round 16 the fun started early with Thompson and Menu clashing early on lap one. A Honda wheel was broken and Thompson spun out. The safety car came out to allow the Accord to be shifted and on the re-start five laps later, Menu and Rydell swapped bodywork (for the third time in less than two competitive laps) on the run through Duffus Dip. Both slewed out of control, but continued down the field, though Menu later retired. Rydell too suffered disappointment when his door swung open and he was black-flagged. Anthony Reid had taken up third place, but having defended his place successfully from Tarquini on a number of occasions, he eventually succumbed when Tarquini's most violent passing move flattened the Nissan's exhaust and strangled the engine.

So, in the end it was Tarquini who took the final podium place, though he also picked up a £500 fine for his part in Reid's demise. Menu too was on the bad boy's list, taking a £1000 fine for his antics with Rydell.

Clockwise from above: Knockhill sees touring cars at their best. Rydell's hopes in the second race were wrecked by his door opening. Can you recognise these famous football stars?

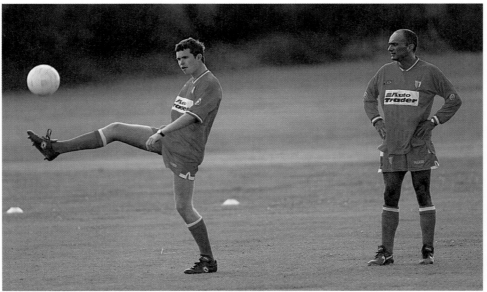

Heavyweight champions

Audi had started the year as the undisputed reigning champions, but knew they had little chance of successfully defending their crowns. The extra 30kg weight penalty the 4WD A4 quattros were hit with during 1996 may have been just right to bring alive that year's title battle, but without the Ingolstadt company having spent much effort developing their machine in the off-season, while the likes of Renault, and Honda made huge strides forward, it left them uncompetitive for 1997. As early as Silverstone, Audi were complaining that the weight penalty was too high, even though, as TOCA boss Alain Gow quite rightly pointed out, at the same point the previous year Audi had said it was too early to talk about adding weight.

'The problem is we need to lose more than 30kg to become competitive again,' claimed Biela early in the season. 'TOCA has the power to decide who wins a championship, and I don't like it if it decides not to do anything until after six or eight meetings. That way there is no way to win the championship.'

Ultimately, Audi had lost the extra 30kg by Oulton Park in May, and promptly became competitive enough for Biela to notch second place in the title chase. The FIA's decision to ban 4WD cars in 1998 will certainly end all controversy in the future about the performance advantages of having such a system. It will also give Audi the chance to prove that they can, or cannot, produce a competitive two-wheel drive car and become the 'light-weight' champions of Super Touring.

Above: Audis lead the way as Menu and Rydell come to blows.
Left: The Audi A4 may not have been a match for Renault at many tracks, but at Knockhill it was in a class of its own

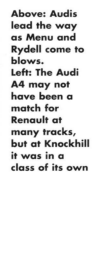

	ROUND 15	35 LAPS	ROUND 16	40 LAPS
	DRIVER	**CAR**	**DRIVER**	**CAR**
1	John BINTCLIFFE	Audi A4 quattro	Frank BIELA	Audi A4 quattro
2	Frank BIELA	Audi A4 quattro	John BINTCLIFFE	Audi A4 quattro
3	Alain MENU	Renault Laguna	Gabriele TARQUINI	Honda Accord
4	Rickard RYDELL	Volvo S40	Kelvin BURT	Volvo S40
5	Anthony REID	Nissan Primera	Jason PLATO	Renault Laguna
6	James THOMPSON	Honda Accord	John CLELAND	Vauxhall Vectra
7	Gabriele TARQUINI	Honda Accord	Rickard RYDELL	Volvo S40
8	Kelvin BURT	Volvo S40	Patrick WATTS	Peugeot 406
9	Will HOY	Ford Mondeo	Tim HARVEY	Peugeot 406
10	John CLELAND	Vauxhall Vectra	Robb GRAVETT	Honda Accord

Fastest lap Frank BIELA
Total Cup Robb GRAVETT

Fastest lap Frank BIELA
Total Cup Robb GRAVETT

Menu crowned at last

After three years as BTCC runner-up, Alain Menu finally won the crown at Snetterton. But he could not stop Williams Renault team-mate Jason Plato taking his maiden victory

Left: The waiting was finally over for Alain Menu as he crossed the line to secure the BTCC title. Above: Grid girl glamour, touring car style

75

Snetterton was where the Williams Renault squad's great season reached its finest moment. Alain Menu clinched the drivers' championship, and at the same time Jason Plato scored his first BTCC race win as the pair took another one-two in round 18.

The closest opposition came from the Hondas and Anthony Reid's Nissan. Reid really had the Primera flying in qualifying, lining up second for the first race and setting a time good enough for pole for the second. Reid's speed flattered to deceive, however, with a

clutch problem sidelining him after just one lap on race one and his 'pole' time for the second disallowed when the Primera failed a ride-height test.

Honda's pace was a little more durable. In the first race Thompson lost two seconds to Menu in the first lap as he sat behind the failing Nissan of Reid, but then gradually closed in to just half a second behind the flying Laguna. That was as close as he got though and Menu eased away again before the flag to win. That victory effectively gave Menu the title, but a last lap move by Frank Biela to pass Jason Plato and take third place

Above: The sun shone on Snetterton. Left: All smiles for Menu and Williams. Right: Radisich, 100 not out

Left: Menu gets away cleanly at the start of the first race. Later in the day, he would be crowned champion

160 mph, we'll soon put a stop to that.

Contact AP Racing for details of the best Brakes & Clutches. For Road or Race.

Tel: 01203 639595 Fax: 01203 639559

meant the Swiss had to score one more point to make it safe.

Round 18 was Plato's. He led all the way with Menu right behind. Towards the end it looked as though there might be a serious challenge from Honda. This time it was Gabriele Tarquini who led the Accord charge and he got close enough in the closing laps to give Menu a little tap - 'normal for an Italian,' said Menu; 'A present to celebrate the title,' added Tarquini – but at the flag the two Renaults were still in front and the drivers' title was emphatically Menu's with six rounds left to run. 'I've worked

bloody hard over the years to win this,' said Menu, 'and now I've done it. I'll sleep well tonight.'

Of the rest, Plato had taken fourth place in round 17 ahead of Rickard Rydell's Volvo and Paul Radisich in the Ford Mondeo, which showed its best form for some time both in qualifying and the race. While in round 18, Thompson finished fourth after dropping away from his team-mate when a vibration set in. Rydell showed consistency with another fifth place and David Leslie salvaged something for Nissan with sixth place.

Top: Jason Plato raced to his maiden win, but the day belonged to a pursuing Alain Menu. Above: Anthony Reid was on-form for Nissan, but disqualified from pole

	ROUND 17	23 LAPS	ROUND 18	23 LAPS
	DRIVER	**CAR**	**DRIVER**	**CAR**
1	Alain MENU	Renault Laguna	Jason PLATO	Renault Laguna
2	James THOMPSON	Honda Accord	Alain MENU	Renault Laguna
3	Frank BIELA	Audi A4 quattro	Gabriele TARQUINI	Honda Accord
4	Jason PLATO	Renault Laguna	James THOMPSON	Honda Accord
5	Rickard RYDELL	Volvo S40	Rickard RYDELL	Volvo S40
6	Paul RADISICH	Ford Mondeo	David LESLIE	Nissan Primera
7	John CLELAND	Vauxhall Vectra	Will HOY	Ford Mondeo
8	Tim HARVEY	Peugeot 406	Kelvin BURT	Volvo S40
9	David LESLIE	Nissan Primera	Frank BIELA	Audi A4 quattro
10	Will HOY	Ford Mondeo	Anthony REID	Nissan Primera

Fastest lap Alain MENU
Total Cup Lee BROOKES

Fastest lap Alain MENU
Total Cup Matt NEAL

Renault cleans up on Audi's day

Audi maintained its great record at Thruxton with wins for both Frank Biela and John Bintcliffe, but it was smiles all round at Renault and Williams as they sealed up the manufacturers' and teams' titles

Above: Bintcliffe leads team mate Biela as they hop the kerbs on the way to a one-two. Right: Start time and the Audis are already making progress

Audi's John Bintcliffe and Frank Biela took the race wins in rounds 19 and 20 at Thruxton as Renault and Williams completed a clean-sweep of the championship's major spoils by clinching the manufacturers' and teams' titles to add to Alain Menu's drivers' crown.

The first of the day's two races was held on a track rapidly drying after a very wet morning. The two Audis, led by third qualifier Bintcliffe, predictably blitzed the opposition at the start, while poleman Rickard Rydell blew it with a poor start and the wrong tyre-choice (intermediates). With Menu also out of contention after a loose rear wheel damaged a disc on the warm-up lap, it was left to the two Hondas of James

Thompson (very quick in qualifying) and Gabriele Tarquini to shadow the Audis and hope they took each other out.

That never happened, but Frank Biela certainly convinced the crowd at the Club chicane that it might with a series of attempts to unsettle his junior colleague. There was contact on several occasions, but Bintcliffe kept his cool to take a fine win, just ahead of Biela.

Will Hoy gave Ford its best result of the year so far, correctly choosing to start on slicks like the top four and moving past a number of fading intermediate runners (including team mate Paul Radisich) to finish fifth. Tim Harvey took an excellent sixth for Peugeot, moving up through the field after pitting on the green flag lap to

Right: Biela takes the flag to win round 20. **Below:** Biela, Menu and Thompson battle at Club. **Bottom:** Harvey and Watts made contact on-track in race two

change intermediates for slicks.

In race two the track was dry, but Biela still had no problem converting second on the grid into an early lead. Poleman Thompson was also out-gunned by Menu. These three soon broke away from the pack. Menu hassled Biela early on, but by lap 15, the Williams crew had seen enough and told him to ease off to ensure he collected enough points to clinch the teams'

crown. Thompson faded, unable to match the mid to late-race pace, but still took his second third place of the day, again ahead of team mate Tarquini.

Bintcliffe moved up from seventh on the grid to take fifth place this time, after moving past a hectic race-long scrap between Rydell's Volvo and Jason Plato's Renault. A last corner sort-out saw Rydell briefly sixth, but Plato took the place back before the line.

ROUND 19	20 LAPS	ROUND 20	20 LAPS
DRIVER	**CAR**	**DRIVER**	**CAR**
1 John BINTCLIFFE	Audi A4 quattro	Frank BIELA	Audi A4 quattro
2 Frank BIELA	Audi A4 quattro	Alain MENU	Renault Laguna
3 James THOMPSON	Honda Accord	James THOMPSON	Honda Accord
4 Gabriele TARQUINI	Honda Accord	Gabriele TARQUINI	Honda Accord
5 Will HOY	Ford Mondeo	John BINTCLIFFE	Audi A4 quattro
6 Tim HARVEY	Peugeot 406	Jason PLATO	Renault Laguna
7 Jason PLATO	Renault Laguna	Rickard RYDELL	Volvo S40
8 David LESLIE	Nissan Primera	Derek WARWICK	Vauxhall Vectra
9 Derek WARWICK	Vauxhall Vectra	Will HOY	Ford Mondeo
10 Lee BROOKES	Peugeot 406	David LESLIE	Nissan Primera

Fastest lap Gabriele TARQUINI
Total Cup Lee BROOKES

Fastest lap Frank BIELA
Total Cup Lee BROOKES

THE ELF REFINERY

**For all your racing fuel and oil requirements contact
Ray Hayward on the Elf / Silverstone Hotline 01327 857 923.**

THE ELF STATION

For every day driving needs visit your local Elf station.

Biela closes on his goal

Frank Biela and Rickard Rydell won the races. Rydell's was Volvo's first of 1997 and Biela's success put him right on course for second in the drivers' points after Jason Plato crashed

Above: James Thompson pleases the fans as an admirer looks on. Right: Frank Biela heads Alain Menu in the first race, before the Swiss driver slowed down to let Williams team mate Jason Plato through for more crucial points

Frank Biela took a big step forward in his bid to be second in the drivers' points as Jason Plato suffered a character building round 22. With qualifying arrangements radically changed, the second race offered opportunities to those prepared to take a gamble and Rickard Rydell seized his chance to take Volvo's first 1997 win.

Saturday's activities had been cancelled due to the funeral of Diana, Princess of Wales, and it had been decided that the fastest race laps in round 21 would set the grid for round 22. That had a big effect on both races, with those who felt they had no chance in the first race treating it as a qualifying session and so relegating the frontrunners in that race to less good grid slots for round 22.

Frank Biela led away in round 21 with team mate John Bintcliffe close behind, chased by Alain Menu. Biela's rival for the runner-up slot, Plato, was fighting his way up the field from fifth place. On lap two he barged past Gabriele Tarquini's Honda and was followed through by James Thompson. His next run-in was with Thompson who picked up a puncture and spun out. That left Jason free to reel in the top three. Menu had moved past Bintcliffe and challenged Biela for several laps, without success. Plato too had little trouble moving past

Top: James Thompson heads for the wall after a brush with Jason Plato punctured one of his Michelins. **Above:** Rickard Rydell took an accomplishjed win for Volvo. **Above left:** Plato's brush with the barrier in round 22

Esso

Esso Ultron

Faster, cleaner protection – right from the start

Bintcliffe and, just before the flag, Menu let him through to second place.

Meanwhile the likes of Anthony Reid and Rickard Rydell had been concentrating on their grid slots for round 22. Reid, who had blown an engine early in the single 15-minute qualifying session, was in and out of the pits throughout the race, putting on new tyres and concentrating on that one hot lap. He took the pole, while Rydell surrendered fifth place in race one to slap on some new tyres and take third place on the grid for race two.

Reid led away at the start of round 22, but Rydell was in determined mood and jumped him at Clearways on the second lap to take a lead he would keep to the flag. Reid was equally comfortable in second place. Meanwhile Thompson had missed out big time. Slow out of Clearways on the first lap, he was jumped by Paul Radisich in the Mondeo and Menu at Paddock. Plato tried to follow them through at Druids, but the pair clashed leaving Thompson in the barrier and Plato hit with a fine. Plato was himself out a couple of laps later after a clash with David Leslie.

Menu eventually slipped past Radisich to take third place, but Paul held on to an excellent fourth place to give Ford its best result since 1995.

Top: Rickard Rydell enjoyed Volvo's only win of the season. Above left: Derek Warwick signs for the usual big Brands crowd. Above right: On the grid there was a minute's silence in memory of Diana, Princess of Wales

ROUND 21	38 LAPS	ROUND 22	38 LAPS
DRIVER	**CAR**	**DRIVER**	**CAR**
1 Frank BIELA	Audi A4 quattro	Rickard RYDELL	Volvo S40
2 Jason PLATO	Renault Laguna	Anthony REID	Nissan Primera
3 Alain MENU	Renault Laguna	Alain MENU	Renault Laguna
4 John BINTCLIFFE	Audi A4 quattro	Paul RADISICH	Ford Mondeo
5 Tim HARVEY	Peugeot 406	Frank BIELA	Audi A4 quattro
6 David LESLIE	Nissan Primera	Kelvin BURT	Volvo S40
7 Will HOY	Ford Mondeo	Gabriele TARQUINI	Honda Accord
8 Patrick WATTS	Peugeot 406	David LESLIE	Nissan Primera
9 Lee BROOKES	Peugeot 406	Tim HARVEY	Peugeot 406
10 Robb GRAVETT	Honda Accord	Patrick WATTS	Peugeot 406

Fastest lap Anthony REID
Total Cup Lee BROOKES

Fastest lap Rickard RYDELL
Total Cup Lee BROOKES

Menu thwarts Plato

A move by Alain Menu cost team mate Jason Plato his chance to be second in the drivers' championship. Frank Biela took the place after an unusually extrovert last BTCC drive

Renault domination was back again for the final round with both cars on the podium in both races, but all was not well in the Didcot camp, because a move by Alain Menu on Jason Plato in the first race ensured that any slim chance the Englishman still had to beat Frank Biela to second in the drivers' points was gone.

Plato had led away with Menu behind and Anthony Reid's Nissan third. For much of the race it looked as though Plato's wishes would come true, but Reid was always a threat and Menu decided to make a move on Plato before

Reid tried to make one on him. 'It was always heading for a sort-out,' said Reid later. 'And it worked in my favour.' That's because when Menu passed Plato into Becketts his team mate ran wide and Reid shot past to take second place.

That's the way it stayed to the flag and Biela's eighth place was enough to guarantee him second in the points.

After the break between races, in which the tension in the Williams-Renault camp was humming, Plato beat poleman Menu away from the line and then drove a solid defensive race to win round 24. Menu was second ahead of

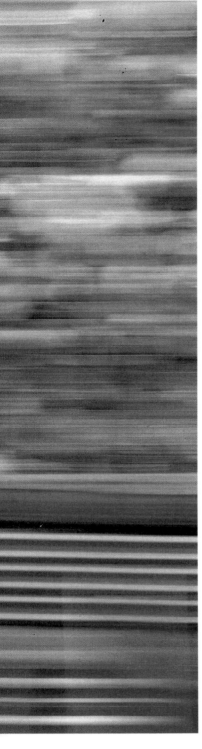

Clockwise from bottom left: Renaults lead off the grid. Gravett secured the Total Cup. Midfield fun from Radisich's Ford, Leslie's Nissan and the Volvos of Rydell and Burt. There was plenty for Renault to celebrate, though Menu was less than cheerful after round 24. End-of-season high-jinks from the teams included role (and attire) swaps for mechanics and grid girls and stone-age car races. The pit-lane walkabout thrives

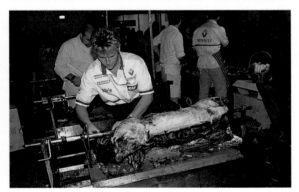

When team mates fall out...

'I think it's quite stupid,' Frank Biela said at Silverstone's final round. His scorn was directed at the tactics of Williams Renault Dealer Racing as it surrendered the small chance Jason Plato had to beat Biela to second place in the championship, by declining to impose team orders.

Alain Menu's decision to take the lead from his team-mate in the first race ultimately meant that Biela's eighth place was enough to deny Plato the runner-up slot in the points And after the final race the one-point margin between the two seemed to give the Menu move great significance.

The reality was a little different. In truth, Plato's chance of beating Biela was not good, even with two race wins. Biela was happy to admit after the race that had he still needed points he would have driven a very different final race, settling for points rather than enjoying a fun final fight - so the one-point margin is something of a red herring.

The nub of the matter is that over the closing races of the season, Plato had started to look as though he might be able to match his team leader. And he had been confidently telling the press just that.

To Menu that was like a red rag to a bull and there was little doubt that given the chance he would at least attempt to put the record straight. That's why Menu made his move, and why he looked, after failing to beat Plato in round 24, perhaps even more upset than Plato had after the previous race.

The row soon passed - in the face of so much success, this was really small beer - but it certainly sets up a fascinating start to 1998.

Gabriele Tarquini's Honda. Reid had again been a contender, but this time his move on James Thompson to try to take third place, though briefly successful, cost him a puncture and also delayed Thompson. James nevertheless kept fourth place ahead of Radisich, who had defended his fifth place with great spirit from a host of faster cars in one of the best midfield melees of the season.

Meanwhile the Total Cup for Independents had finally gone the way of Robb Gravett's Honda. The fight had gone down to the wire with both Peugeot driver Lee Brookes and BMW rookie Colin Gallie in contention to the end, but eventually a couple of conservative points–gathering drives from Gravett clinched the title for which he'd been the favourite since he joined the fray for round three.

It had been a suitably dramatic finale for the series and though the happy atmosphere at Renault had been momentarily soured, there was no spoiling its superb record over the season or denying that, as at the first meeting of the year and so many others in the course of the season, the Laguna was the class of the field.

ROUND 23	17 LAPS	**ROUND 24**	20 LAPS
DRIVER	**CAR**	**DRIVER**	**CAR**
1 Alain MENU	Renault Laguna	Jason PLATO	Renault Laguna
2 Anthony REID	Nissan Primera	Alain MENU	Renault Laguna
3 Jason PLATO	Renault Laguna	Gabriele TARQUINI	Honda Accord
4 Gabriele TARQUINI	Honda Accord	James THOMPSON	Honda Accord
5 Kelvin BURT	Volvo S40	Paul RADISICH	Ford Mondeo
6 David LESLIE	Nissan Primera	David LESLIE	Nissan Primera
7 James THOMPSON	Honda Accord	Rickard RYDELL	Volvo S40
8 Frank BIELA	Audi A4 quattro	Kelvin BURT	Volvo S40
9 Patrick WATTS	Peugeot 406	Patrick WATTS	Peugeot 406
10 Paul RADISICH	Ford Mondeo	Will HOY	Ford Mondeo

Fastest lap Anthony REID
Total Cup Matt NEAL

Fastest lap Alain MENU
Total Cup Matt NEAL

RENAULT LAGUNA

IT'S ALL WORKED OUT BEAUTIFULLY ON ROAD AND TRACK

BTCC 1997 TRIPLE CHAMPIONS
WINNERS OF THE DRIVERS', MANUFACTURERS' AND TEAMS' CHAMPIONSHIPS

RENAULT

Canny Gravett grabs the cash

BTCC veteran Robb Gravett took full advantage of the new dropped-score points system to lift the biggest portion of the £250,000 Total Cup prize fund at the last round

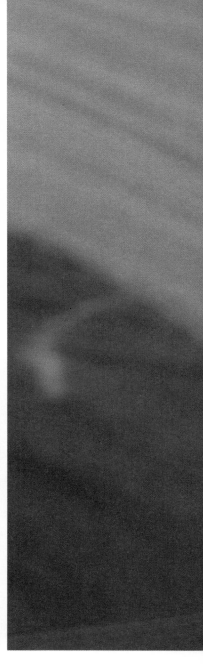

Above: Tug-of-love for Neal, Brookes Wall, and Gallie, but Gravett (right) got custody. Far right Team Dynamics disasters with Nissan (top) and Ford

Robb Gravett grabbed the Total Cup for Independents at the last round, though in truth his claim to the £75,000 first prize was a strong one throughout the year.

It had been a respectable rather than a dramatic season for the non-works runners, certainly more competitive than it had been in 1997, but not quite what TOCA and Total looked for when they increased the prize money and re-vamped the rules over the winter.

Gravett had shrewdly picked probably the best equipment in the field – a 1996 MSD-built Honda Accord, but his victory was never a foregone conclusion. The 1990 overall BTCC champion joined the party at the second meeting with an Accord that had done service with German series team Linder in 1996.

When news of his impending arrival on the scene first broke in the week before round three of the championship at Silverstone, Gravett cautiously intimated that his debut was not yet

certain; that it depended on how the Accord went in the short time he had to test it. That it was quick straight out of the box was clear when he did indeed show at Silverstone and won both races, even dipping into the main championship points in round four.

From then, it was clear that Robb was going to be able to play a tactical game, concentrating on collecting points. The Gravett/Accord combo was not always the quickest, but it was among the quickest everywhere and it was reliable. By the time the final rounds arrived, Gravett had won the Independents' class six times and scored good points in all but two of the races he'd entered and, although he was apparently behind on points, the new-for-'97 dropped scores system in fact gave him a solid advantage.

He did not falter at that final meeting, doing only what he needed to clinch the title and the big cash prize.

Gravett's closest opponents in the points race were '96 champion Lee

Brookes and series newcomer Colin Gallie. Ultimately it was Brookes who came closest. Having overcome early-season reliability problems with his ex-works Peugeot 406, Lee won nine times, but couldn't match Gravett's consistency.

Gallie by contrast showed admirable consistency, but by the end of the season his BMW 320i was beginning to show its

Above: The Gravett Accord was quick, consistent and well-driven. Left: Gallie won the opening rounds. Far left: Good learning year for Wall

age. Colin led the points almost all season, starting out with two wins at the first meeting to celebrate his BTCC debut – and his recent wedding. A further win came later at Oulton Park, but his impressive first season at this level didn't quite net him the top prize, indeed he had to be content with third place.

The other two regulars in the class,

Matt Neal and Jamie Wall, had to be content with the scraps, but both had performed well on occasion. Neal's season was an ambitious and eventful one. He started the year in a brand new Ford Mondeo, designed and built by Team Dynamics. It showed promise, but not reliability. The Mondeo brought Matt two wins at Thruxton, but he abandoned

it mid-season for a Nissan Primera. This too was a very quick bit of kit, but sadly no great paragon of reliability either. Ultimately the season brought Matt six wins, but little sign of the works chance his speed suggests he deserves.

Wall was the youngest man in the field and came to the BTCC with no great pedigree, but he certainly didn't disgrace

himself. The Mint Motorsport Cavalier was a year or more older than the three cars which did most of the winning, but it was generally reliable and although Wall won no races he did a competent job.

The final entrant was Ian Heward, whose Cavalier is now well past its best. He didn't appear at every round and when he did, he generally failed to qualify. Six points – for being the fifth of five finishers at Donington, was the only score Heward managed.

The range of changes to the Total Cup instituted at the beginning of the season brought a slight improvement to the class, but not the hoped-for boom. At the end of the season, Total completed its BTCC stint, but TOCA is confident that a new sponsor can be found to back the Independents in 1998. The real trick will be to attract more entrants to the series and persuade them they have a real chance of fighting with the slower works cars and so putting themselves into contention for paid drives.

Brabhams save BMW's Bathurst

Geoff and David Brabham won the first Super Touring edition of Bathurst's great race after their team mates had been thrown out

The switch of the 'Great Race' Bathurst 1000 to Super Touring rules this year ensured a healthy dose of BTCC cars made the trip halfway across the globe, but it was the local teams that came out on top after a thrilling encounter including incident, controversy and a post-race exclusion.

Few knew what to expect when the BTCC teams mixed it with the local boys, but for those who had witnessed Williams Renault's domination of the British series this season, it came as no surprise to see the Laguna, driven by Jason Plato who teamed-up with Alain Menu, storm away at the start of the race after overtaking pole-sitter Paul

Morris with a stunning move around the outside into the BP Cutting.

Such was the pace of the Renault that some thought it was running with a light fuel load, but that proved not to be the case when it came in after a longer than average stint for refuelling and a handover to Menu. That left Morris in front, only for a puncture to cut short his stint just one lap later.

That incident left Menu with around a 30 second lead over the field and it seemed that nothing could stop the Laguna adding a victory at Bathurst to its BTCC title successes. Nothing, except a safety car that is.

Ironically, Menu's sister car, driven by

Alan Jones, had gone off at the BP Cutting. 'It was a mongrel patch of oil,' said the former World Champion. 'I just came up through the Cutting, hit the oil and understeered into the fence.'

Two further safety car periods, one of which occured for questionable reasons, always prevented the Renault gaining any kind of decent advantage and the fact that Menu and Plato were both having to push hard certainly played a part in the Laguna's ultimate demise.

During the second hour of the race, Menu started to complain that his brake pedal was getting long and that a pad-change would be required at half distance. A problem with the right front

pad, allied to the fact been negated, meant t lap down into fifth sp

But once back on t was again setting an in taking four seconds pe leading BMWs and A still to go, it seemed t in the Renault camp t made a mistake at Mc bouncing the car acros brilliant recovery, and stopped with a differe

This left the Audis McConville, sharing w Hemroulle, and Frank with Brad Jones, at the

Above: The Brabham boys head for glory. Top left: A plethora of international stars. Right: Runners-up Biela and Jones

made their final stop they dropped to third and fourth, although both moved up one place again when Geoff Brabham pitted in the BMW.

With 19 laps to go, Craig Baird in the leading BMW pitted for the final time, importantly not handing over to team-mate Morris, and rejoined ahead of Biela.

Three laps later, David Brabham, sharing with his brother, collided with Hemroulle at the BP Cutting. Both cars spun and forced the safety car out as they blocked the track. After pitting briefly for damage repair they rejoined with Hemroulle ahead, although it did not take long for Brabham to grab third and, with six laps to go, he moved past Biela

for second at Repco.

Unfortunately for the former BTCC driver, Baird was far enough ahead to take the chequered flag in front, but four hours later his car would be disqualified because it was found the New Zealander had exceeded the maximum permissible time in the cockpit. That handed victory to the Brabham duo, with Biela's Audi second and Hemroulle's third.

Of the remainder of the BTCC bunch, Rickard Rydell took fourth place for Volvo after a consistent drive with Jim Richards. Derek Warwick, sharing with Aussie hero Peter Brock, grabbed sixth, despite losing 12 laps when they had to replace a driveshaft.

Double top TT for Renault

Alain Menu won the £25,000 RAC Tourist Trophy at Donington, from team mate Jason Plato and Volvo's Rickard Rydell. A novel three-race format, with one reversed grid, plus a handful of visiting drivers, set-up an entertaining season-closer. Nissan's Anthony Reid was closest to Menu for speed and won a heat, but was just sixth in the final, while Frank Biela bowed out with fourth

Above: Plato chases heat one winner Reid. Left Aaron Slight leads a heat one gaggle down the Craners as Neal spins in the background. Below left: Menu cracks just one more bottle of bubbly. Below right: Bike ace Slight brought a breath of fresh air to the TT, but his race mileage was short

Above: The Christian Abt (left) and Kris Nissen Audis visited. Far left: Yvan Muller gave the front-drive A4 a competitive debut. Left Fog didn't spoil it

Audi Sport UK

It may not have matched the triumphs of the 1996 season, but this year's campaign was a good one for Audi Sport's Buckingham-based UK offshoot.

The early races were the low point with top driver Frank Biela quick to point out that little if any development had been carried out on the four-wheel drive A4 over the winter as Audi Sport in Germany concentrated on the front-driver it will have to use from next year, but gradually developments both from Audi and from tyre supplier Dunlop improved matters. The loss, at Oulton Park at the end of May, of the 30kg extra weight penalty the A4 quattro had picked up midway through last year was

another bonus. Add in the odd wet or damp race or qualifying session and the campaign was back on track

By the second half of the year Biela – engineered as last year by the experienced Roger King in one of only three completely new A4 quattros built for 1997 was in contention for second place in the championship. Team mate John Bintcliffe had matured into a consistent challenger to his team leader, working well with a new race engineer this year – ex-ROC Audi man Rafael Campillos - on his re-vamped '96 car.

In the end the team finished the year with seven wins – compared to 14 for Renault, two for Honda and one for

Volvo – and Biela took second place in the drivers' championship. Not a bad swansong for the quattro in the UK.

Although the reliability record was not quite perfect, as it had been in '96, it was still very good and the Audi Sport UK team under John Wickham, though still only in its second year, still merits a place in the top echelon of BTCC teams.

ENGINE/GEARBOX

TYPE IN-LINE FOUR CYLINDER, DOHC, 16-VALVE, ALLOY BLOCK/ALLOY HEAD **MOUNTING** LONGITUDINAL **CAPACITY** 1998CC **TRANSMISSION** FOUR-WHEEL DRIVE AUDI/HEWLAND LONGITUDINAL, SEQUENTIAL-SHIFT GEARBOX, 6-SPEED PLUS REVERSE

BODY

MODEL AUDI A4 QUATTRO, 4 DOOR **LENGTH** 4479MM **WIDTH** 1753MM **HEIGHT** 1311MM **WHEELBASE** 2610MM **WEIGHT** 1070KG/1040KG

SUSPENSION

FRONT DOUBLE WISHBONES, COILSPRINGS, GAS-FILLED DAMPERS, ANTI-ROLL BAR **REAR** DOUBLE WISHBONES, COILSPRINGS GAS-FILLED DAMPERS, ANTI-ROLL BAR **BRAKES** VENTILATED DISCS, FOUR-PISTON CALIPERS FRONT, FOUR-PISTON CALIPERS REAR **WHEELS** 8.2 X 19-INCH **TYRES** DUNLOP

Team Mondeo

It was another character building season for the men at Ford, although at least this year there did appear to be light at the end of the tunnel by the end of the year, and Will Hoy even notched up a podium place (third) in one of the heats at the Tourist Trophy.

The unloved, late-commissioned and rush-built, 1996 Schubel Mondeos were this year replaced with Reynard-designed and built cars, but again the programme ran late. The cars were among the last to appear and for most of the first half of the season there weren't enough spares or development parts to make any meaningful testing possible.

However in the second half of the

season there were a few more smiles to be seen on the faces of the members of Dick Bennetts's West Surrey Racing crew which was again entrusted with running the race programme.

At Snetterton Paul Radisich looked to be on for a qualifying time in the top three, but instead crashed out. However there were a couple of good race results before the end of the season. Hoy and engineer Greg Wheeler made the right tyre call in the damp at Thruxton and Will came in fifth, while at Brands Radisich, who was engineered by Will

Phillips, ran third for much of round 22, before finishing fourth.

Engine improvements arrived at regular intervals from Cosworth, but the car was still happier on momentum tracks, where it did not have to drag out of slow corners up long straights and although its race pace was pretty good its biggest problem remained to the end of the year the inability to put in a really good 'hot' qualifying lap.

This winter will be a crucial one with a promising base to work from and Ford promising its most serious effort yet.

ENGINE/GEARBOX

TYPE SIX-CYLINDER, 60-DEGREE VEE, DOHC, 24-VALVE, ALLOY BLOCK/ALLOY HEAD **MOUNTING** TRANSVERSE **CAPACIT**Y 2000CC
TRANSMISSION FRONT-WHEEL DRIVE REYNARD/XTRAC SEQUENTIAL-SHIFT GEARBOX, 6-SPEED PLUS REVERSE

BODY

MODEL FORD MONDEO GHIA 2.0I 5 DOOR **LENGTH** 4556MM **WIDTH** 1745MM **HEIGHT** 1425MM **WHEELBASE** 2704MM **WEIGHT** 975KG

SUSPENSION

FRONT MACPHERSON STRUT, LOWER WISHBONE, GAS-FILLED DAMPERS, ANTI-ROLL BAR **REAR** MACPHERSON STRUT, PARALLEL ARMS, FORWARD LINK, COILSPRINGS, GAS-FILLED DAMPERS, ANTI-ROLL BAR **BRAKES** VENTILATED DISCS, SIX-PISTON CALIPERS FRONT, FOUR-PISTON CALIPERS, REAR **WHEELS** 8 X 19-INCH **TYRES** MICHELIN

Our favourite Circuit

Speed, reliability and teamwork. That's what it takes to be No.1 in Touring Cars. And that's what it takes to be No.1 in international express deliveries. Which is why DHL are sponsors of race-days featuring the Auto Trader RAC Touring Car Championship. So if you've got an urgent delivery, you can rely on us to win the race.

DHL
WORLDWIDE EXPRESS ®

We keep your promises

Team Honda Sport

It was a season full of largely unfulfilled promise for the Honda squad. The Accord programme had been switched over the winter from Motor Sport Developments to Prodrive, which immediately embarked on a ground-up re-design for the Accord, which, with its very powerful Neil Brown-built engines and wishbone suspension all-round, is still reckoned to be the BTCC contender which should go best.

Keith Knott's new car was immediately quick, with James Thompson the closest of the Renault-challengers at Donington's Easter season-opener, but over the course of the year a handful of mechanical problems, a handful of driver errors and a few bits of plain bad luck kept Thompson and Gabriele Tarquini down in fifth and sixth places in the drivers' points, although third in both manufacturers' and teams' tables were more satisfying.

The good times came with a pair of

wins – one for each driver. Tarquini, engineered by former Dunlop tyre man Spencer Deakin triumphed in the damp at Thruxton in May, and Thompson, who was engineered by Peter Harrison, took his turn a fortnight later at Brands Hatch, when the pair took an excellent one-two. It was one weekend when Honda looked to have the measure of the rest and later in the season they looked the pick of the bunch at Croft,

but were unable to capitalise through a mixture of bad luck and driver error. The dire weather forced a grid based on championship positions making the drivers to fight through traffic and then both pilots made errors when poised to challenge leader Alain Menu.

With this gelling year under team manager Dave Benbow behind it the Honda team should be even more of a force in 1998.

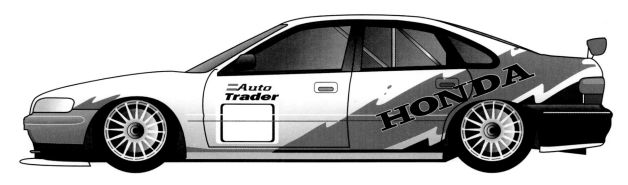

ENGINE/GEARBOX

TYPE IN-LINE FOUR CYLINDER, DOHC, 16-VALVE, ALLOY HEAD/ALLOY BLOCK **MOUNTING** TRANSVERSE **CAPACITY** 1998CC **TRANSMISSION** FRONT-WHEEL DRIVE PRODRIVE/HEWLAND SEQUENTIAL-SHIFT GEARBOX, 6-SPEED PLUS REVERSE

BODY

MODEL HONDA ACCORD 2.0I LS 4 DOOR **LENGTH** 4685MM **WIDTH** 1720MM **HEIGHT** 1380MM **WHEELBASE** 2720MM **WEIGHT** 975KG

SUSPENSION

FRONT DOUBLE WISHBONES, COIL SPRINGS, GAS-FILLED DAMPERS, ANTI-ROLL BAR **REAR** DOUBLE WISHBONES, COIL SPRINGS, GAS-FILLED DAMPERS, ANTI-ROLL BAR **BRAKES** VENTILATED DISCS, EIGHT-PISTON CALIPERS, FRONT TWO-PISTON CALIPERS, REAR **WHEELS** 8.2 X 19-INCH **TYRES** MICHELIN

'Ayufit?'

'De do chor'

'Aye-aye' **Fit like?**

'Ye're fine?' 'Hellooo'

'Ciamar a thathu'

'Whit laike'

'How's it guin?'

'Si' thee'

Bout ya

'Why-aye man!'

'Hi, how ya doin?'

'Aareet Pet?'

What about yer?

Noo ba

'Is that yerself?'

'Ay oop'

'Yaa reet?' 'Ow-ard-a?'

Top of the morn'n

'Yawlrite-Kidda?'

'Naa-den'

'Yawlrite-like?'

'Ow doo?'

Bore da

'Ello mi duck' 'Ey, up!'

'T'nawn da' 'Gid mawnin-g-each'

'Sut mae?' **Aawwrighht?**

'Watch 'eer'

Iechyd da 'Salve'

'Yu awl right, boy?'

'Nos da' 'Daarling' **Hi ya!**

'Ow are yer?'

'Aw right?'

'Ow be gwain?'

Wotcha!

'Alright my 'ansome?' 'Hello old bean'

'Ow 'e diddlin?' 'Allo my luvver' **'Hi'**

for the mobile phone network with
the best UK digital coverage,
the word is ◯ **vodafone**

Vodafone Nissan Racing

Very impressive comeback season for Nissan in the BTCC. There was a new shape for the Primera and a completely re-organised team.

By the end of the year drivers David Leslie and Anthony Reid had notched up five podium finishes and shown winning potential – indeed Reid did win one of the heats at the end-of-season, non-championship Tourist Trophy.

The new venture was a joint operation between Nissan Motorsports Europe, under touring car supremo Alec Poole, and Ray Mallock Ltd (switching from Vauxhall). The idea was that NME should be responsible for design and build and RML for running the cars and development programme. In practice, with the rush to get the new cars up and running and NME's top design man Richard Divilla busy in Japan working on Skyline GT cars, Ray Mallock's operation at Wellingborough took the lead on design and build.

Although it was the last of the 1997 BTCC cars to appear, many of the parts had already been tested on interim '96-shelled cars, and the new Nissan was quick right from the off. Leslie was fourth in round one and already on the podium in round three.

Race engineers Phil Barker and Stuart Ayling, along with Divilla, soon had the chassis working well and the engine – which had been entrusted this season to John Judd's Engine Developments concern was generally reckoned to be one of the very best in the field.

It was a season full of promise and great things must be expected in 1998.

ENGINE/GEARBOX

TYPE IN-LINE FOUR CYLINDER, DOHC, 16-VALVE, ALLOY HEAD/ALLOY BLOCK **MOUNTING** TRANSVERSE **CAPACITY** 1998CC
TRANSMISSION FRONT-WHEEL DRIVE RML/XTRAC SEQUENTIAL-SHIFT GEARBOX, 6-SPEED PLUS REVERSE

BODY

MODEL NISSAN PRIMERA GT 4-DOOR **LENGTH** 4400MM **WIDTH** 1700MM **HEIGHT** 1395MM **WHEELBASE** 2550MM **WEIGHT** 975KG

SUSPENSION

FRONT DOUBLE WISHBONES, COIL SPRINGS, GAS-FILLED DAMPERS, ANTI-ROLL BAR **REAR** MACPHERSON STRUT, COILSPRINGS
ANTI-ROLL BAR **BRAKES** VENTILATED DISCS, SIX-PISTON CALIPERS, FRONT, TWO-PISTON CALIPERS, REAR
WHEELS 8 X 19-INCH **TYRES** MICHELIN

Esso Ultron Team Peugeot

Peugeot's BTCC programme had undergone a radical re-think for 1997. Gone was the last genuine factory-run works team, as Peugeot motorsport manager Mick Linford

bowed to the inevitable and contracted the running of the cars out to a specialist team, Motor Sport Developments.

Having lost the deal to run the Hondas at the end of 1996, MSD picked up another car with great potential, the 406. The promise was fulfilled on a couple of occasions, but this was ultimately a rather patchy season with occasional weekends when the 406 was simply off the pace.

It was a learning year for the team and Peugeot's budget, though improved over that in year's past, is still some way short of that deployed by most of the other manufacturers. The decision to re-design the car and build a completely new one for '97 should reap dividends in the end, but it did mean a pretty slow start to the season, although Tim Harvey's opportunistic second place in changing conditions at Thruxton provided the team with a big boost.

Harvey's second runner-up slot of the year at Donington Park in June was even more encouraging, coming, as it did, in the dry and with no other fluke factor.

The experience gained by the team under MSD boss David Whitehead should be invaluable for '98. It's a tight and efficient unit with Paul Risbridger as team manager and Eddie Hinckley leading the race engineering team. With a full winter's test and development programme on a car, which should just

need updating for next season, 1998 will be the crucial year for the partnership. Then it must deliver. Maybe Linford and Whitehead will even stop having to answer the recurring question – how come it can't win here when it's dominant in Germany?

ENGINE/GEARBOX

TYPE IN-LINE FOUR CYLINDER, DOHC, 16-VALVE, ALLOY HEAD/ALLOY BLOCK **MOUNTING** TRANSVERSE **CAPACITY** 1998CC **TRANSMISSION** FRONT-WHEEL DRIVE MSD/XTRAC SEQUENTIAL-SHIFT GEARBOX, 6-SPEED PLUS REVERSE

BODY

MODEL PEUGEOT 406 4-DOOR **LENGTH** 4546MM **WIDTH** 1752MM **HEIGHT** 1240MM **WHEELBASE** 2668MM **WEIGHT** 975KG

SUSPENSION

FRONT MACPHERSON STRUTS, COIL SPRINGS, GAS-FILLED DAMPERS, ANTI-ROLL BAR, REAR MULTI-LINK TRAILING ARM MACPHERSON STRUTS, COIL SPRINGS, GAS-FILLED DAMPERS, ANTI-ROLL BAR **BRAKES** VENTILATED DISCS, 2 X FOUR-PISTON CALIPERS FRONT, FOUR-PISTON CALIPERS, REAR **WHEELS** 8.25 X 19-INCH **TYRES** MICHELIN

Williams Renault Dealer Racing

A brilliant season for the Didcot–based Williams Renault squad. The cars were quick everywhere, quickest of all at most circuits, and, just as importantly, very reliable. This was the third year of the Williams Renault touring car partnership and the operation is now very slick indeed.

There were a few structural changes at the beginning of the season, with highly respected Belgian Didier Debae joining as team manager after team director Ian Harrison and team manager Dick Goodman moved on. Debae moved into the job from Schubel Engineering in Germany. On the technical side things were fairly stable with John Russell still leading the design and engineering squad and Mark Ellis engineering Menu as he has since 1995. The 1997 version of the Laguna which was a refined version of the '96 (first full-Williams) car appeared earlier than most of its rivals and showed a worthwhile improvement in speed right from its first tests.

With Greg Wheeler moving to Ford along with Will Hoy, a new engineer was needed for new driver Jason Plato and Jerry Hughes, fresh from Ray Mallock Ltd and Vauxhall, where he worked with James Thompson, filled that role successfully. By the end of the year the pair were working very well together and Plato's speed in relationship to Menu's confirmed that.

Champion Alain Menu's finishing record is something any team could be proud of – he only failed to finish once and that was down to accident damage. A major part in achieving that great reliability record was played by engine builder Sodemo. Last year the French firm's motors attracted a great deal of criticism for their unreliability. This year the improvement was immense. Sodemo's engines produced a lot more power – they were generally a match for all but the Honda's and – the reliability was excellent.

ENGINE/GEARBOX

TYPE IN-LINE FOUR CYLINDER, DOHC, 16-VALVE, ALLOY HEAD/IRON BLOCK **MOUNTING** TRANSVERSE **CAPACITY** 1998CC
TRANSMISSION FRONT-WHEEL DRIVE WILLIAMS/HEWLAND SEQUENTIAL-SHIFT GEARBOX 6-SPEED PLUS REVERSE

BODY

MODEL RENAULT LAGUNA 2.0 RT 4-DOOR **LENGTH** 4508MM **WIDTH** 1752MM **HEIGHT** 1433MM **WHEELBASE** 2670MM **WEIGHT** 975KG

SUSPENSION

FRONT MACPHERSON STRUTS, COIL SPRINGS, GAS-FILLED DAMPERS, ANTI-ROLL BAR **REAR** TRAILING ARM, TORSION BARS, COILSPRINGS
GAS-FILLED DAMPERS, ANTI-ROLL BAR **BRAKES** VENTILATED DISCS, SIX-PISTON CALIPERS, FRONT FOUR PISTON CALIPERS, REAR
WHEELS 8.3 X 19-INCH **TYRES** MICHELIN

Vauxhall Sport

Vauxhall picked up the wooden spoon in the manufacturers' championship and it sometimes seemed hard to remember that just two year's earlier John Cleland had won the championship for the Luton marque.

No one had really expected fireworks from the Vectras this year, after they'd been switched from Ray Mallock Ltd to the brand new Triple Eight Race Engineering concern, but equally no one had expected it to be this bad. Neither Cleland nor Derek Warwick made it into the top 10 in the drivers' points and a handful of fifths were the best results.

The problems were many – from the need to start the year with lightly re-worked '96 cars, to a disastrous German-designed aerodynamic package, to the simple problems of getting a new organisation up and running efficiently. The personnel list was a good one with former Williams Touring Car Engineering team director Ian Harrison taking up a similar role here and John Gentry switching from TWR to head-up the engineering strength and bringing Dave Kelly with him. Harrison and Gentry were two of the new company's directors, the others being Warwick and Roland Dane – a long-time business associate of Warwick's and the man who

ran the Park Lane Racing BTCC team a couple of years back.

Further re-worked cars arrived mid-season and were an improvement, but the team still reckoned that the aero kit (which the German teams had dropped, but BTCC rules would not allow Triple Eight to) was holding them back.

The mix remains the same for 1998 and, with relations with Opel Motorsport now much improved following Volker Strycek's appointment as its boss, a much better season is in prospect. Certainly no one can afford another year like this one.

ENGINE/GEARBOX

TYPE IN-LINE FOUR CYLINDER, DOHC, 16-VALVE, ALLOY HEAD/IRON BLOCK **MOUNTING** TRANSVERSE **CAPACITY** 1998CC **TRANSMISSION** FRONT-WHEEL DRIVE XTRAC SEQUENTIAL-SHIFT GEARBOX, 6-SPEED PLUS REVERSE

BODY

MODEL VAUXHALL VECTRA 4-DOOR **LENGTH** 4477MM **WIDTH** 1707MM **HEIGHT** 1310MM **WHEELBASE** 2640MM **WEIGHT** 975KG

SUSPENSION

FRONT MACPHERSON STRUTS, LOWER WISHBONES, ANTI-ROLL BAR **REAR** TWIN LATERAL LINKS AND TRAILING ARM, COAXIAL SPRING/DAMPER & TRAILING ARM, ANTI-ROLL BAR **BRAKES** VENTILATED DISCS, SIX-PISTON CALIPERS, FRONT FOUR PISTON CALIPERS, REAR **WHEELS** 9 X 19-INCH **TYRES** MICHELIN

Volvo S40 Racing

The S40's debut year brought some success, but a good deal less than the TWR-run Volvo operation had come to expect with its old 850s. Both at the beginning and the end of the season the S40 challenge was strong, but for much of the middle part of the year it was a team of nearly men.

Roger Silman continued as team director as did team manager Ken Page, but there were upheavals in the design and engineering department following John Gentry's move to Triple Eight and Vauxhall shortly after the S40 prototype had been completed. Brendan Gribben, who had co-operated with Gentry on the initial design moved from his back-room position to the race team and Graham Taylor joined from Audi as race engineer. Initially all seemed to be going smoothly, with TWR's usual comprehensive winter test programme making the S40 a pre-season favourite. Rydell then finished second in three of

the first four races to establish himself firmly as Alain Menu's closest early-season challenger.

After that though the team found it hard to keep the car right on the pace. Much of this was simply down to the process of learning how the new car worked – it is an entirely different machine to its predecessor, with improved aerodynamics and better base rear suspension on the plus side, but a much smaller footprint (narrower track and shorter wheelbase).

The car's race pace was usually pretty

good, but hot qualifying laps were hard to come by and the clutch of Rydell poles we've been used to were reduced to just one at Thruxton, while Kelvin Burt came very close to putting it in the number one slot at Donington. Rydell's win eventually came at Brands Hatch, partly thanks to that weekend's unconventional qualifying procedures.

TWR reckons it knows what it has to do to make the car into the consistent winner it wants and it has the winter to sort the S40 out and prove it a worthy successor to the 850 in 1998.

ENGINE/GEARBOX

TYPE IN-LINE FIVE CYLINDER, DOHC, 20-VALVE, ALLOY HEAD/ALLOY BLOCK **MOUNTING** TRANSVERSE **CAPACITY** 1999CC **TRANSMISSION** FRONT-WHEEL DRIVE TWR/XTRAC SEQUENTIAL-SHIFT GEARBOX, 6-SPEED PLUS REVERSE

BODY

MODEL VOLVO S40 4-DOOR SALOON **LENGTH** 4670MM **WIDTH** 1760MM **HEIGHT** 1430MM **WHEELBASE** 2670MM **WEIGHT** 975KG

SUSPENSION

FRONT MACPHERSON STRUTS, GAS-FILLED DAMPERS, ANTI-ROLL BAR **REAR** DELTA-LINK, SEMI-INDEPENDENT, LONGITUDINAL TRAILING ARMS, GAS-FILLED DAMPERS, COILSPRINGS, ANTI-ROLL BAR **BRAKES** VENTILATED DISCS, EIGHT-PISTON CALIPERS FRONT, TWO-PISTON CALIPERS, REAR **WHEELS** 8.2 X 19-INCH **TYRES** MICHELIN

Rock-It Cargo

Robb Gravett teamed up with Graham Hathaway Racing to run his Ex-Team Linder Honda Accord from the second meeting of the year and lifted the top Total Cup prize.

The Accord proved to be the ideal Independents' weapon, quick and reliable and both team and driver made the best of it. The 1990 overall BTCC Champion's budget was adequate, but not big enough to allow him the luxury of chasing after the works boys to score psychological points at the potential risk of serious car damage.

Robb instead set out to win the Total Cup and his focussed and effective campaign produced the desired result.

Brookes Motorsport

Lee Brookes defended his Total Cup title in an ex-works Peugeot 406 and made the '96 Pug, which hadn't exactly excelled for the factory, into a potent contender by the end of the year.

The 406 suffered reliability problems early in the year, but the professional Brookes Motorsport outfit, in which Lee's father Jon also plays a major role had it going very well by the end of the year to mount a serious last minute challenge for the title.

Despite winning most races – nine to Gravett's six – Brookes had to be content with second in the points.

Team Dynamics

Richard Kaye moved into Steve Neal's Team Dynamics set-up as team manager and Matt Neal started the year with a new Ford Mondeo, designed and built in-house.

In the early part of the season the Mondeo did not excel, struggling for pace and reliability, but the team gradually improved it to a point where it looked ready to run consistently at the front, before a much better manufacturer-support deal prompted a switch to a Nissan Primera.

The Primera was predictably quick, but it too struggled on reliability. Ultimately Neal won as many races (six) as champion Gravett, but on consistency, he was nowhere.

Team DCRS

Newcomer Colin Gallie was an impressive addition to the Total Cup field and indeed he led the points table for most of the season.

Driving a 1994-built BMW 320i run by long-time touring car specialist Dave Cook - the man responsible for Vauxhall's BTCC programmes from 1989 to '93 - he was a consistent and quick performer, although the BMW was a little too long in the tooth to live with the Gravett, Brookes and Neal cars.

Three wins - two at the opening meeting weren't quite enough although finishes in all but two events - an engine blew at Brands Hatch - speak volumes for the job Cook's team did.

Mint Motorsport

Brian Ellis and Paul Andrew again brought their Vauxhall Cavalier to the party. Replacing title contender Richard Kaye in the driving seat was youngster Jamie Wall.

Wall's background was in one-make racing, but he adadpted well to the Super Touring car, though never really looking likely to challenge the likes of Gravett and Brookes for a win.

The Cavalier was perhaps capable of a little better, but even when it was put in the hands of Tim Sugden - on a one-off drive in the end-of-season Tourist Trophy - it was no match for Matt Neal's Team Dynamics Ford Mondeo.

The Rest

PRO-MOTOR SPORT

Ian Heward's ageing 1993 Vauxhall Cavalier was out-classed last year and this year things were no better. On the occasions when he showed, the likeable midlander generally failed to qualify.

JAN BRUNSTEDT

Swedish airline pilot/owner Brunstedt brought his ex-RML Vectra over for the second meeting of the year, but trailed home last and lapped in each race.

DONINGTON PARK - MARCH 30-31

QUALIFYING TIMES - ROUND 1

1	Jason PLATO	1:36.327	11	Gabriele TARQUINI	1:37.84
2	Alain MENU	1:36.423	12	Tim HARVEY	1:37.848
3	Rickard RYDELL	1:36.517	13	Derek WARWICK	1:37.884
4	James THOMPSON	1:36.930	14	Paul RADISICH	1:37.945
5	Kelvin BURT	1:37.122	15	John BINTCLIFFE	1:38.132
6	David LESLIE	1:37.176	16	John CLELAND	1:38.894
7	Anthony REID	1:37.239	17	Lee BROOKES	1:40.187
8	Frank BIELA	1:37.355	18	Matt NEAL	1:41.017
9	Will HOY	1:37.730	19	Jamie WALL	1:41.197
10	Patrick WATTS	1:37.757	20	Colin GALLIE	1:41.901

RESULTS - ROUND 1

18 LAPS; 45.00 MILES

	Driver	Car	Race time	Best lap
1	Alain MENU	Renault Laguna	29:36.777	1:37.084
2	Jason PLATO	Renault Laguna	29:39.919	1:37.234
3	Kelvin BURT	Volvo S40	30:01.018	1:38.341
4	David LESLIE	Nissan Primera	30:01.297	1:38.443
5	John BINTCLIFFE	Audi A4 quattro	30:07.318	1:38.893
6	Paul RADISICH	Ford Mondeo	30:12.451	1:38.985
7	Gabriele TARQUINI	Honda Accord	30:15.615	1:38.996
8	Patrick WATTS	Peugeot 406	30:15.959	1:39.715
9	Derek WARWICK	Vauxhall Vectra	30:16.127	1:39.170
10	Tim HARVEY	Peugeot 406	30:21.563	1:39.064

11. John CLELAND (Vauxhall Vectra) 30:21.743, 12. Colin GALLIE (BMW 320i) 31:20.320
13. Jamie WALL (Vauxhall Cavalier) 15 laps
NOT CLASSIFIED
Rickard RYDELL (Volvo S40), Lee BROOKES (Peugeot 406), Will HOY (Ford Mondeo), Anthony REID (Nissan Primera), James THOMPSON (Honda Accord), Frank BIELA (Audi A4 quattro), Matt NEAL (Ford Mondeo)

QUALIFYING TIMES - ROUND 2

1	Jason PLATO	1:36.293	11	Paul RADISICH	1:37.815
2	Alain MENU	1:36.420	12	Derek WARWICK	1:37.872
3	James THOMPSON	1:36.440	13	Patrick WATTS	1:37.890
4	Rickard RYDELL	1:36.602	14	John BINTCLIFFE	1:37.890
5	Frank BIELA	1:37.115	15	Will HOY	1:37.932
6	Kelvin BURT	1:37.249	16	John CLELAND	1:38.605
7	Gabriele TARQUINI	1:37.300	17	Lee BROOKES	1:40.427
8	Anthony REID	1:37.447	18	Matt NEAL	1:40.647
9	Tim HARVEY	1:37.458	19	Jamie WALL	1:40.685
10	David LESLIE	1:37.565	20	Colin GALLIE	1:41.684

RESULTS - ROUND 2

18 LAPS; 45.00 MILES

1	Alain MENU	Renault Laguna	29:49.841	1:37.570
2	Rickard RYDELL	Volvo S40	29:52.207	1:38.546
3	Frank BIELA	Audi A4 quattro	29:54.110	1:38.555
4	Gabriele TARQUINI	Honda Accord	29:55.348	1:38.546
5	John BINTCLIFFE	Audi A4 quattro	30:01.530	1:38.887
6	James THOMPSON	Honda Accord	30:04.288	1:38.035
7	Paul RADISICH	Ford Mondeo	30:10.089	1:38.965
8	Derek WARWICK	Vauxhall Vectra	30:12.124	1:39.353
9	Kelvin BURT	Volvo S40	30:13.473	1:38.876
10	Colin GALLIE	BMW 320i	31:10.630	1:42.272

11. David LESLIE (Nissan Primera) 31:44.804, 12. Matt NEAL (Ford Mondeo) 13 laps
NOT CLASSIFIED Jamie WALL (Vauxhall Cavalier), Tim HARVEY (Peugeot 406), Jason PLATO (Renault Laguna), Lee BROOKES (Peugeot 406), Patrick WATTS (Peugeot 406), Anthony REID (Nissan Primera), John CLELAND (Vauxhall Vectra) **DID NOT START** Will Hoy (Ford Mondeo)

SILVERSTONE - APRIL 19-20

QUALIFYING TIMES - ROUND 3

1	Jason PLATO	1:22.607	12	John CLELAND	1:24.187
2	Alain MENU	1:22.819	13	Paul RADISICH	1:24.352
3	James THOMPSON	1:22.884	14	Will HOY	1:24.493
4	Gabriele TARQUINI	1:23.003	15	John BINTCLIFFE	1:24.590
5	Rickard RYDELL	1:23.119	16	Patrick WATTS	1:24.606
6	Kelvin BURT	1:23.429	17	RobB GRAVETT	1:25.309
7	Tim HARVEY	1:23.604	18	Lee BROOKES	1:25.684
8	David LESLIE	1:23.796	19	Colin GALLIE	1:26.970
9	Frank BIELA	1:24.019	20	Jamie WALL	1:27.007
10	Derek WARWICK	1:24.051	21	Matt NEAL	1:27.532
11	Anthony REID	1:24.105	22	Jan BRUNSTEDT	1:27.890

RESULTS - ROUND 3

20 LAPS; 50.40 MILES

1	Alain MENU	Renault Laguna	28:20.191	1:24.004
2	Rickard RYDELL	Volvo S40	28:20.895	1:23.908
3	David LESLIE	Nissan Primera	28:33.207	1:24.252
4	Kelvin BURT	Volvo S40	28:35.457	1:24.357
5	Gabriele TARQUINI	Honda Accord	28:40.711	1:24.132
6	John CLELAND	Vauxhall Vectra	28:41.160	1:24.887
7	Frank BIELA	Audi A4 quattro	28:43.555	1:25.186
8	Derek WARWICK	Vauxhall Vectra	28:46.910	1:24.958
9	Patrick WATTS	Peugeot 406	28:47.270	1:25.192
10	Jason PLATO	Renault Laguna	28:55.617	1:23.257

11. Tim HARVEY (Peugeot 406) 28:59.973, 12. Will HOY (Ford Mondeo) 29:03.723, 13. Robb GRAVETT (Honda Accord) 29:16.484, 14. Lee BROOKES (Peugeot 406) 29:19.160, 15. Colin GALLIE (BMW 320i) 19 laps, 16. Jamie WALL (Vauxhall Cavalier) 19 laps, 17. Jan BRUNSTEDT (Opel Vectra) 19 laps. **NOT CLASSIFIED** James THOMPSON (Honda Accord), Anthony REID (Nissan Primera), John BINTCLIFFE (Audi A4 quattro), Paul RADISICH (Ford Mondeo), Matt NEAL (Ford Mondeo).

QUALIFYING TIMES - ROUND 4

1	Alain MENU	1:22.625	12	Tim HARVEY	1:24.092
2	James THOMPSON	1:22.916	13	David LESLIE	1:24.109
3	Jason PLATO	1:22.960	14	Paul RADISICH	1:24.271
4	Gabriele TARQUINI	1:23.165	15	John CLELAND	1:24.522
5	Rickard RYDELL	1:23.229	16	John BINTCLIFFE	1:24.553
6	Kelvin BURT	1:23.762	17	Robb GRAVETT	1:25.358
7	Anthony REID	1:23.972	18	Lee BROOKES	1:25.844
8	Derek WARWICK	1:24.007	19	Matt NEAL	1:26.633
9	Patrick WATTS	1:24.028	20	Jamie WALL	1:27.227
10	Will HOY	1:24.029	21	Colin GALLIE	1:27.468
11	Frank BIELA	1:24.049	22	Jan BRUNSTEDT	1:28.160

RESULTS - ROUND 4

20 LAPS; 50.40 MILES

1	Alain MENU	Renault Laguna	28:13.133	1:23.428
2	Rickard RYDELL	Volvo S40	28:16.320	1:23.494
3	Jason PLATO	Renault Laguna	28:18.855	1:23.544
4	Tim HARVEY	Peugeot 406	28:39.609	1:24.800
5	Derek WARWICK	Vauxhall Vectra	28:42.383	1:24.890
6	John CLELAND	Vauxhall Vectra	28:43.344	1:24.893
7	Will HOY	Ford Mondeo	28:48.055	1:24.821
8	Patrick WATTS	Peugeot 406	28:48.852	1:24.809
9	James THOMPSON	Honda Accord	28:58.492	1:23.793
10	Robb GRAVETT	Honda Accord	29:09.574	1:25.763

11. Lee BROOKES (Peugeot 406) 29:15.418, 12. Colin GALLIE (BMW 320i), 29:29.891, 13. Jamie WALL (Vauxhall Cavalier) 29:34.289, 14. Jan BRUNSTEDT (Opel Vectra) 19 laps, 15. Gabriele TARQUINI (Honda Accord) 19 laps
NOT CLASSIFIED
David LESLIE (Nissan Primera), John BINTCLIFFE (Audi A4 quattro), Frank BIELA (Audi A4 quattro), Anthony REID (Nissan Primera), Paul RADISICH (Ford Mondeo), Kelvin BURT (Volvo S40)

THRUXTON - MAY 4-5

QUALIFYING TIMES - ROUND 5

1	Alain MENU	1:16.850	12	Will HOY	1:18.805
2	Jason PLATO	1:17.433	13	Anthony REID	1:19.065
3	Gabriele TARQUINI	1:17.521	14	Patrick WATTS	1:19.088
4	Frank BIELA	1:17.704	15	Derek WARWICK	1:19.240
5	James THOMPSON	1:17.704	16	John CLELAND	1:19.624
6	John BINTCLIFFE	1:18.287	17	Robb GRAVETT	1:20.580
7	Paul RADISICH	1:18.323	18	Matt NEAL	1:20.631
8	Rickard RYDELL	1:18.373	19	Colin GALLIE	1:21.781
9	David LESLIE	1:18.680	20	Jamie WALL	1:22.337
10	Kelvin BURT	1:18.764	21	Lee BROOKES	1:23.128
11	Tim HARVEY	1:18.770			

RESULTS - ROUND 5

18 LAPS; 42.48 MILES

1	Frank BIELA	Audi A4 quattro	27:03.695	1:25.976
2	Gabriele TARQUINI	Honda Accord	27:07.230	1:27.216
3	Alain MENU	Renault Laguna	27:09.621	1:25.751
4	John BINTCLIFFE	Audi A4 quattro	27:10.668	1:23.948
5	Rickard RYDELL	Volvo S40	27:20.230	1:28.256
6	James THOMPSON	Honda Accord	27:20.535	1:23.749
7	David LESLIE	Nissan Primera	27:27.555	1:25.978
8	Anthony REID	Nissan Primera	27:30.148	1:25.609
9	Tim HARVEY	Peugeot 406	27:47.668	1:29.060
10	Paul RADISICH	Ford Mondeo	27:52.312	1:28.995

11. Will HOY (Ford Mondeo) 27:56.398, 12. Patrick WATTS (Peugeot 406), 28:01.258, 13. Matt NEAL (Ford Mondeo) 28:13.676, 14. John CLELAND (Vauxhall Vectra) 28:19.594, 15. Derek WARWICK (Vauxhall Vectra) 28:25.852, 16. Robb GRAVETT (Honda Accord) 17 laps 17. Colin GALLIE (BMW 320i) 17 laps, 18. Jamie WALL (Vauxhall Cavalier) 13 laps.
NOT CLASSIFIED
Lee BROOKES (Peugeot 406), Kelvin BURT (Volvo S40), Jason PLATO (Renault Laguna)

QUALIFYING TIMES - ROUND 6

1	Alain MENU	1:16.538	12	Anthony REID	1:18.336
2	Gabriele TARQUINI	1:17.183	13	Kelvin BURT	1:18.374
3	James THOMPSON	1:17.368	14	John CLELAND	1:18.388
4	Jason PLATO	1:17.462	15	Tim HARVEY	1:18.510
5	John BINTCLIFFE	1:17.473	16	Will HOY	1:18.521
6	Frank BIELA	1:17.658	17	Robb GRAVETT	1:19.995
7	David LESLIE	1:17.868	18	Matt NEAL	1:20.410
8	Patrick WATTS	1:17.897	19	Lee BROOKES	1:21.183
9	Paul RADISICH	1:18.185	20	Jamie WALL	1:21.356
10	Derek WARWICK	1:18.197	21	Colin GALLIE	1:21.706
11	Rickard RYDELL	1:18.233			

RESULTS - ROUND 6

22 LAPS; 51.92 MILES

1	Gabriele TARQUINI	Honda Accord	34:12.672	1:18.848
2	Tim HARVEY	Peugeot 406	34:13.359	1:20.546
3	Alain MENU	Renault Laguna	34:17.121	1:18.824
4	Anthony REID	Nissan Primera	34:18.984	1:20.452
5	Rickard RYDELL	Volvo S40	34:24.918	1:19.618
6	Derek WARWICK	Vauxhall Vectra	34:29.934	1:20.464
7	Jason PLATO	Renault Laguna	34:33.469	1:18.807
8	John BINTCLIFFE	Audi A4 quattro	34:33.594	1:19.072
9	John CLELAND	Vauxhall Vectra	34:38.043	1:20.513
10	Paul RADISICH	Ford Mondeo	34:38.801	1:19.626

11. David LESLIE (Nissan Primera) 34:42.266, 12. Will HOY (Ford Mondeo) 34:47.859, 13. Kelvin BURT (Volvo S40) 21 laps, 14. Matt NEAL (Ford Mondeo) 21 laps, 15. Colin GALLIE (BMW 320i) 21 laps, 16. Robb GRAVETT (Honda Accord) 21 laps, 17 Jamie WALL (Vauxhall Cavalier) 20 laps
NOT CLASSIFIED
James THOMPSON (Honda Accord), Patrick WATTS (Peugeot 406), Frank BIELA (Audi A4 quattro).

BRANDS HATCH - MAY 17-18

QUALIFYING TIMES - ROUND 7

1	Alain MENU	44.826
2	Jason PLATO	44.845
3	James THOMPSON	44.916
4	Gabriele TARQUINI	44.994
5	Anthony REID	45.007
6	David LESLIE	45.046
7	Will HOY	45.300
8	Frank BIELA	45.310
9	Patrick WATTS	45.315
10	Rickard RYDELL	45.340
11	Paul RADISICH	45.400
12	Kelvin BURT	45.446
13	John BINTCLIFFE	45.511
14	Derek WARWICK	45.579
15	John CLELAND	45.746
16	Matt NEAL	46.096
17	Lee BROOKES	46.119
18	Robb GRAVETT	46.155
19	Jamie WALL	46.785
20	Colin GALLIE	47.464
21	Tim HARVEY	1:11.101

RESULTS - ROUND 7   38 LAPS; 45.60 MILES

1	Alain MENU	Renault Laguna	29:07.076	45.107
2	James THOMPSON	Honda Accord	29:11.856	45.158
3	Jason PLATO	Renault Laguna	29:12.270	45.220
4	David LESLIE	Nissan Primera	29:12.567	45.215
5	Anthony REID	Nissan Primera	29:12.780	45.196
6	Gabriele TARQUINI	Honda Accord	29:13.011	45.350
7	Rickard RYDELL	Volvo S40	29:22.917	45.318
8	Kelvin BURT	Volvo S40	29:23.385	45.331
9	Frank BIELA	Audi A4 quattro	29:23.878	45.610
10	Derek WARWICK	Vauxhall Vectra	29:24.903	45.724

11. John CLELAND (Vauxhall Vectra) 29:26.442, 12. Robb GRAVETT (Honda Accord) 29:52.784, 13. Lee BROOKES (Peugeot 406) 37 laps, 14. Jamie WALL (Vauxhall Cavalier) 37 laps, 15. Matt NEAL (Ford Mondeo) 20 laps.

NOT CLASSIFIED
Patrick WATTS (Peugeot 406), John BINTCLIFFE (Audi A4 quattro), Tim HARVEY (Peugeot 406), Paul RADISICH (Ford Mondeo), Will HOY (Ford Mondeo). **DID NOT START** Colin Gallie (BMW 320 i).

QUALIFYING TIMES - ROUND 8

1	Gabriele TARQUINI	44.909
2	James THOMPSON	44.939
3	Alain MENU	44.959
4	Anthony REID	45.112
5	Jason PLATO	45.240
6	Rickard RYDELL	45.256
7	David LESLIE	45.309
8	Paul RADISICH	45.393
9	John BINTCLIFFE	45.416
10	Kelvin BURT	45.428
11	Will HOY	45.478
12	Patrick WATTS	45.627
13	Frank BIELA	45.635
14	Derek WARWICK	45.784
15	John CLELAND	45.996
16	Robb GRAVETT	46.177
17	Matt NEAL	46.343
18	Lee BROOKES	46.536
19	Jamie WALL	46.920
20	Tim Harvey	no time
21	Colin Gallie	no time

RESULTS - ROUND 8   38 LAPS; 45.60 MILES

1	James THOMPSON	Honda Accord	29:03.363	44.922
2	Gabriele TARQUINI	Honda Accord	29:08.624	44.935
3	David LESLIE	Nissan Primera	29:12.104	45.027
4	Alain MENU	Renault Laguna	29:16.499	44.907
5	Jason PLATO	Renault Laguna	29:16.900	45.132
6	Frank BIELA	Audi A4 quattro	29:19.737	45.251
7	Paul RADISICH	Ford Mondeo	29:22.393	45.174
8	Kelvin BURT	Volvo S40	29:23.292	45.186
9	John CLELAND	Vauxhall Vectra	29:23.733	45.728
10	Tim HARVEY	Peugeot 406	29:27.311	45.664

11. Derek WARWICK (Vauxhall Vectra) 29:28.044, 12. John BINTCLIFFE (Audi A4 quattro) 29:30.029, 13. Robb GRAVETT (Honda Accord) 29:40.385, 14. Anthony REID (Nissan Primera) 29:45.241, 15. Lee BROOKES (Peugeot 406) 37 laps, 16. Rickard RYDELL (Volvo S40) 37 laps, 17. Will HOY (Ford Mondeo) 37 laps

NOT CLASSIFIED
Patrick WATTS (Peugeot 406), Jamie WALL (Vauxhall Cavalier). **DID NOT START** Colin Gallie (BMW 320 i), Matt Neal (Ford Mondeo).

OULTON PARK - MAY 25-26

QUALIFYING TIMES - ROUND 9

1	Alain MENU	58.849
2	Jason PLATO	59.278
3	Frank BIELA	59.322
4	Gabriele TARQUINI	59.346
5	James THOMPSON	59.412
6	Kelvin BURT	59.532
7	Paul RADISICH	59.600
8	Will HOY	59.758
9	John BINTCLIFFE	59.835
10	David LESLIE	59.914
11	Tim HARVEY	59.946
12	John CLELAND	1:00.033
13	Derek WARWICK	1:00.091
14	Patrick WATTS	1:00.150
15	Robb GRAVETT	1:00.647
16	Matt NEAL	1:00.767
17	Lee BROOKES	1:00.976
18	Jamie WALL	1:01.924
19	Colin GALLIE	1:02.079
20	Rickard RYDELL	time disallowed
21	Anthony REID	time disallowed

RESULTS - ROUND 9   30 LAPS; 49.50 MILES

1	Alain MENU	Renault Laguna	33:18.677	59.615
2	Jason PLATO	Renault Laguna	33:21.332	59.941
3	Frank BIELA	Audi A4 quattro	33:24.663	1:00.735
4	John BINTCLIFFE	Audi A4 quattro	33:30.813	1:00.705
5	John CLELAND	Vauxhall Vectra	33:37.118	1:00.767
6	Rickard RYDELL	Volvo S40	33:37.418	1:00.424
7	Anthony REID	Nissan Primera	33:37.740	1:00.859
8	Paul RADISICH	Ford Mondeo	33:38.833	1:00.432
9	Kelvin BURT	Volvo S40	33:39.592	1:00.419
10	David LESLIE	Nissan Primera	33:39.980	1:00.768

11. Derek WARWICK (Vauxhall Vectra) 33:43.178, 12. Colin GALLIE (BMW 320i) 29 laps, 13. Jamie WALL (Vauxhall Cavalier) 28 laps 14. Robb GRAVETT (Honda Accord) 27 laps, 15. Matt NEAL (Ford Mondeo) 26 laps, 16. Lee BROOKES (Peugeot 406) 22 laps.

NOT CLASSIFIED Patrick WATTS (Peugeot 406), Gabriele TARQUINI (Honda Accord), Tim HARVEY (Peugeot 406), James THOMPSON (Honda Accord). **DID NOT START** Will HOY (Ford Mondeo)

QUALIFYING TIMES - ROUND 10

1	Alain MENU	58.909		12	Paul RADISICH	59.799
2	Rickard RYDELL	59.221		13	Derek WARWICK	59.828
3	Jason PLATO	59.251		14	John CLELAND	1:00.185
4	Gabriele TARQUINI	59.300		15	Patrick WATTS	1:00.364
5	James THOMPSON	59.326		16	Robb GRAVETT	1:00.587
6	John BINTCLIFFE	59.499		17	Matt NEAL	1:00.769
7	Kelvin BURT	59.571		18	Lee BROOKES	1:01.538
8	Frank BIELA	59.620		19	Jamie WALL	1:01.915
9	Anthony REID	59.638		20	Colin GALLIE	1:01.972
10	Tim HARVEY	59.737		21	Will HOY	no time
11	David LESLIE	59.756				

RESULTS - ROUND 10   27 LAPS; 44.55 MILES

1	Alain MENU	Renault Laguna	27:25.407	59.668
2	James THOMPSON	Honda Accord	27:31.571	1:00.311
3	Rickard RYDELL	Volvo S40	27:33.587	1:00.021
4	Jason PLATO	Renault Laguna	27:39.779	59.833
5	John BINTCLIFFE	Audi A4 quattro	27:46.809	1:00.704
6	David LESLIE	Nissan Primera	27:52.900	1:00.318
7	Paul RADISICH	Ford Mondeo	27:55.676	1:00.406
8	Tim HARVEY	Peugeot 406	28:11.349	1:01.051
9	Lee BROOKES	Peugeot 406	26 laps	1:01.686
10	Colin GALLIE	BMW 320i	26 laps	1:02.283

11. Jamie WALL (Vauxhall Cavalier) 26 laps, 12. John CLELAND (Vauxhall Vectra), 26 laps, 13. Robb GRAVETT (Honda Accord) 26 laps 14. Matt NEAL (Ford Mondeo) 25 laps 15. Patrick WATTS (Peugeot 406) 23 laps

NOT CLASSIFIED
Kelvin BURT (Volvo S40), Frank BIELA (Audi A4 quattro), Anthony REID (Nissan Primera), Derek WARWICK (Vauxhall Vectra), Gabriele TARQUINI (Honda Accord). **DID NOT START** Will HOY (Ford Mondeo)

DONINGTON PARK - JUNE 14-15

QUALIFYING TIMES - ROUND 11

1	Alain MENU	1:17.534		11	Derek WARWICK	1:19.272
2	Tim HARVEY	1:18.448		12	Gabriele TARQUINI	1:19.404
3	James THOMPSON	1:18.538		13	John CLELAND	1:19.585
4	Jason PLATO	1:18.555		14	Paul RADISICH	1:19.636
5	David LESLIE	1:18.785		15	Patrick WATTS	1:20.058
6	Frank BIELA	1:18.833		16	Lee BROOKES	1:20.480
7	John BINTCLIFFE	1:18.857		17	Matt NEAL	1:20.855
8	Anthony REID	1:19.129		18	Colin GALLIE	1:21.433
9	Will HOY	1:19.161		19	Robb GRAVETT	1:22.436
10	Rickard RYDELL	1:19.200		20	Jamie WALL	1:24.165
11	Kelvin BURT	1:19.218		22	Ian HEWARD	1:28.493

RESULTS - ROUND 11   25 LAPS; 49.00 MILES

1	Frank BIELA	Audi A4 quattro	33:27.982	1:19.619
2	Alain MENU	Renault Laguna	33:28.959	1:19.414
3	John BINTCLIFFE	Audi A4 quattro	33:30.774	1:19.657
4	Jason PLATO	Renault Laguna	33:35.151	1:19.623
5	Rickard RYDELL	Volvo S40	33:36.935	1:19.707
6	James THOMPSON	Honda Accord	33:38.321	1:19.730
7	Tim HARVEY	Peugeot 406	33:38.919	1:19.735
8	Kelvin BURT	Volvo S40	33:40.749	1:19.908
9	David LESLIE	Nissan Primera	33:41.616	1:19.507
10	Patrick WATTS	Peugeot 406	33:45.232	1:19.852

11. Anthony REID (Nissan Primera) 33:54.031, 12. John CLELAND (Vauxhall Vectra) 33:55.378, 13. Will HOY (Ford Mondeo) 33:56.166, 14. Lee BROOKES (Peugeot 406) 34:24.497, 15. Colin GALLIE (BMW 320i) 34:36.108, 16. Matt NEAL (Nissan Primera) 34:38.885, 17. Robb GRAVETT (Honda Accord) 24 laps, 18. Jamie WALL (Vauxhall Cavalier) 24 laps.

NOT CLASSIFIED
Gabriele TARQUINI (Honda Accord), Paul RADISICH (Ford Mondeo), Derek WARWICK (Vauxhall Vectra), Ian HEWARD (Vauxhall Cavalier)

QUALIFYING TIMES - ROUND 12

1	Alain MENU	1:10.803		11	Frank BIELA	1:11.633
2	Kelvin BURT	1:10.877		12	David LESLIE	1:11.730
3	Gabriele TARQUINI	1:10.973		13	John CLELAND	1:11.795
4	James THOMPSON	1:11.018		14	Will HOY	1:11.860
5	Jason PLATO	1:11.178		15	Derek WARWICK	1:11.881
6	Tim HARVEY	1:11.386		16	Matt NEAL	1:12.008
7	Rickard RYDELL	1:11.411		17	Robb GRAVETT	1:12.747
8	Paul RADISICH	1:11.520		18	Lee BROOKES	1:12.778
9	John BINTCLIFFE	1:11.543		19	Colin GALLIE	1:13.552
10	Anthony REID	1:11.575		20	Jamie WALL	1:13.868
11	Patrick WATTS	1:11.600		22	Ian HEWARD	1:21.607

RESULTS - ROUND 12   26 LAPS; 50.96 MILES

1	Alain MENU	Renault Laguna	32:13.115	1:11.584
2	Tim HARVEY	Peugeot 406	32:15.132	1:12.055
3	Frank BIELA	Audi A4 quattro	32:15.484	1:12.445
4	John BINTCLIFFE	Audi A4 quattro	32:16.725	1:12.464
5	Patrick WATTS	Peugeot 406	32:38.939	1:12.746
6	Gabriele TARQUINI	Honda Accord	32:42.374	1:11.566
7	Rickard RYDELL	Volvo S40	32:44.274	1:12.668
8	John CLELAND	Vauxhall Vectra	32:44.587	1:13.017
9	Will HOY	Ford Mondeo	32:47.032	1:12.967
10	Derek WARWICK	Vauxhall Vectra	32:54.543	1:13.003

11. James THOMPSON (Honda Accord) 32:54.629, 12. Lee BROOKES (Peugeot 406) 32:58.542, 13. Matt NEAL (Nissan Primera) 33:13.661, 14. Jamie WALL (Vauxhall Cavalier) 33:25.657, 15. Colin GALLIE (BMW 320i) 33:29.947, 16. Ian HEWARD (Vauxhall Cavalier) 22 laps

NOT CLASSIFIED
Anthony REID (Nissan Primera), Kelvin BURT (Volvo S40), Paul RADISICH (Ford Mondeo), David LESLIE (Nissan Primera), Jason PLATO (Renault Laguna), Robb GRAVETT (Honda Accord).

CROFT - JUNE 28-29

GRID - ROUND 13 (CHAMPIONSHIP POSITIONS, NO QUALIFYING - RAIN)

1	Alain MENU		12	Anthony REID
2	Rickard RYDELL		13	Derek WARWICK
3	Jason PLATO		14	Paul RADISICH
4	Frank BIELA		15	Patrick WATTS
5	Gabriele TARQUINI		16	Will HOY
6	James THOMPSON		17	Lee BROOKES
7	John BINTCLIFFE		18	Colin GALLIE
8	David LESLIE		19	Robb GRAVETT
9	Tim HARVEY		20	Jamie WALL
10	Kelvin BURT		21	Matt NEAL
11	John CLELAND			

RESULTS - ROUND 13   25 LAPS; 53.17 MILES

1	Alain MENU	Renault Laguna	35:03.301	1:22.680
2	Jason PLATO	Renault Laguna	35:06.150	1:22.981
3	Rickard RYDELL	Volvo S40	35:06.904	1:23.168
4	Frank BIELA	Audi A4 Quattro	35:07.574	1:23.133
5	James THOMPSON	Honda Accord	35:18.439	1:22.884
6	John CLELAND	Vauxhall Vectra	35:19.630	1:23.571
7	Derek WARWICK	Vauxhall Vectra	35:23.619	1:23.644
8	Will HOY	Ford Mondeo	35:26.672	1:23.531
9	John BINTCLIFFE	Audi A4 Quattro	35:38.815	1:23.668
10	Tim HARVEY	Peugeot 406	35:43.981	1:23.853

11. Patrick WATTS (Peugeot 406) 35:50.695, 12. Kelvin BURT (Volvo S40) 36!4.565, 13. Matt NEAL (Nissan Primera) 24 LAPS, 14. Jamie WALL (Vauxhall Cavalier) 24 laps, 15. Robb GRAVETT (Honda Accord) 24 laps, 16. Colin GALLIE (BMW 320i) 23 laps, Gabriele TARQUINI (Honda Accord) 22 laps.

NOT CLASSIFIED
Lee BROOKES (Peugeot 406), David LESLIE (Nissan Primera), Anthony REID (Nissan Primera), Paul RADISICH (Ford Mondeo)

GRID - ROUND 14 (CHAMPIONSHIP POSITIONS, NO QUALIFYING - RAIN)

1	Alain MENU		12	Anthony REID
2	Rickard RYDELL		13	Derek WARWICK
3	Jason PLATO		14	Paul RADISICH
4	Frank BIELA		15	Patrick WATTS
5	Gabriele TARQUINI		16	Will HOY
6	James THOMPSON		17	Lee BROOKES
7	John BINTCLIFFE		18	Colin GALLIE
8	David LESLIE		19	Robb GRAVETT
9	Tim HARVEY		20	Jamie WALL
10	Kelvin BURT		21	Matt NEAL
11	John CLELAND			

RESULTS - ROUND 14   17 LAPS; 36.04 MILES

1	Alain MENU	Renault Laguna	28:41.470	1:22.048
2	James Thompson	Honda Accord	28:42.413	1:22.100
3	David LESLIE	Nissan Primera	28:42.826	1:22.632
4	Jason PLATO	Renault Laguna	28:43.165	1:22.589
5	John CLELAND	Vauxhall Vectra	28:43.648	1:23.144
6	John BINTCLIFFE	Audi A4 Quattro	28:44.782	1:22.730
7	Tim HARVEY	Peugeot 406	28:45.567	1:23.054
8	Anthony REID	Nissan Primera	28:46.516	1:22.981
9	Rickard RYDELL	Volvo S40	28:47.015	1:22.445
10	Derek WARWICK	Vauxhall Vectra	28:47.799	1:23.146

11. Paul RADISICH (Ford Mondeo) 28:48.485, 12. Kelvin BURT (Volvo S40) 28:48.879, 13 Lee BROOKES (Peugeot 406) 28:50.728, 14. Robb GRAVETT (Honda Accord) 28:50.861, 15. Colin GALLIE (BMW 320i) 28:51.963, 16. Patrick WATTS (Peugeot 406) 28:53.231, 17 Frank BIELA (Audi A4 Quattro) 15 laps

NOT CLASSIFIED Jamie WALL (Vauxhall Cavalier), Gabriele TARQUINI (Honda Accord), Will HOY (Ford Mondeo), Matt NEAL (Nissan Primera)

KNOCKHILL - AUGUST 1-2

QUALIFYING TIMES - ROUND 15

1	John BINTCLIFFE	52.608		12	Patrick WATTS	53.532
2	Frank BIELA	52.715		13	Tim HARVEY	53.567
3	Alain MENU	52.810		14	Derek WARWICK	53.582
4	Rickard RYDELL	52.996		15	John CLELAND	53.788
5	Anthony REID	53.036		16	Robb GRAVETT	54.010
6	James THOMPSON	53.114		17	Lee BROOKES	54.328
7	Gabriele TARQUINI	53.145		18	Matt NEAL	54.402
8	Paul RADISICH	53.178		19	Colin GALLIE	55.046
9	David LESLIE	53.192		20	Jamie WALL	55.333
10	Jason PLATO	53.259		21	Will HOY	57.250
11	Kelvin BURT	53.463				

RESULTS - ROUND 15   35 LAPS; 45.50 MILES

1	John BINTCLIFFE	Audi A4 Quattro	31:46.368	53.568
2	Frank BIELA	Audi A4 Quattro	31:47.089	53.445
3	Alain MENU	Renault Laguna	32:10.838	53.733
4	Rickard RYDELL	Volvo S40	32:13.205	53.966
5	Anthony REID	Nissan Primera	32:13.518	53.853
6	James THOMPSON	Honda Accord	32:13.882	53.797
7	Gabriele TARQUINI	Honda Accord	32:14.319	53.737
8	Kelvin BURT	Volvo S40	32:18.791	54.133
9	Derek WARWICK	Vauxhall Vectra	32:29.480	54.406
10	John CLELAND	Vauxhall Vectra	32:32.119	54.292

11 David LESLIE (Nissan Primera) 32:32.845, 12 Will HOY (Ford Mondeo) 32:42.239, 13 Robb GRAVETT (Honda Accord) 34 laps, 14 Tim HARVEY (Peugeot 406) 34 laps, 15 Colin GALLIE (BMW 320i) 34 laps, 16 Jamie WALL (Vauxhall Cavalier) 34 laps, 17 Lee BROOKES (Peugeot 406) 32 laps, 18 Patrick WATTS (Peugeot 406), 29 laps

NOT CLASSIFIED
Jason PLATO (Renault Laguna), Matt NEAL (Nissan Primera), Paul RADISICH (Ford Mondeo)

How much freight can we handle?

The new name in motor sports freight is the premier name for the International entertainment industry and has been for nearly two decades.

Contact: Graham Gillham or Mark Cahill
Rock-It Cargo Ltd, Delta Way, Egham, Surrey TW20 8RX
Telephone: (01784) 431301 Fax: (01784) 471052
Telex: 8811054 RUSHIN G

Ideal for a drive in the country

There's never been a better time to head straight for the open - with only your Sony in-car CD system for company.

While others might wait with baited breath over the results of the British Open, the results are plain to see in the Sony DJ-C450RDS.

That's short for the very latest in-car CD system featuring a 10 disc CD autochanger, which can be conveniently stashed away in the boot & a high quality radio cassette all controlled either from the front panel or from Sony's revolutionary Joystick remote control.

The RDS bit constantly tunes the radio to the best quality signal, wherever you happen to be in the

country and allows you to receive local

traffic information, interrupting the BBC radio station, cassette or CD you are listening to. Making sure you never end up stuck in the rough.

The rest of the package is no Sunday driver, either. The amp offers 4x35 watts of maximum output power, and you get a host of luxurious finishing touches & useful features.

All in all, an audio package that's well above par - so drive one soon.

SONY

Why compromise?

QUALIFYING TIMES - ROUND 16

1	Frank BIELA	52.451
2	John BINTCLIFFE	52.509
3	James THOMPSON	52.638
4	Alain MENU	52.665
5	Rickard RYDELL	52.785
6	Anthony REID	52.828
7	Gabriele TARQUINI	52.869
8	David LESLIE	53.173
9	Paul RADISICH	53.280
10	Kelvin BURT	53.314
11	Will HOY	53.402
12	Derek WARWICK	53.460
13	Patrick WATTS	53.575
14	John CLELAND	53.581
15	Robb GRAVETT	53.798
16	Matt NEAL	54.077
17	Lee BROOKES	54.087
18	Tim HARVEY	54.109
19	Colin GALLIE	54.807
20	Jason PLATO	1:29.531
21	Jamie WALL	no time

RESULTS - ROUND 16   40 LAPS; 52.00 MILES

1	Frank BIELA	Audi A4 quattro	38:41.554	53.461
2	John BINTCLIFFE	Audi A4 quattro	38:44.541	53.524
3	Gabriele TARQUINI	Honda Accord	39:03.445	53.860
4	Kelvin BURT	Volvo S40	39:10.507	54.088
5	Jason PLATO	Renault Laguna	39:24.610	54.597
6	John CLELAND	Vauxhall Vectra	39:27.756	54.619
7	Rickard RYDELL	Volvo S40	39:28.029	53.971
8	Patrick WATTS	Peugeot 406	39:30.469	54.646
9	Tim HARVEY	Peugeot 406	39:30.629	54.742
10	Robb GRAVETT	Honda Accord	39 laps	54.974

11 Colin GALLIE (BMW 320i) 39 laps, 12 Jamie WALL (Vauxhall Cavalier) 39 laps, 13 Derek WARWICK (Vauxhall Vectra) 39 laps, 14 Will HOY (Ford Mondeo) 39 laps, 15 Lee BROOKES (Peugeot 406) 34 laps,

NOT CLASSIFIED David LESLIE (Nissan Primera), Anthony REID (Nissan Primera), Paul RADISICH (Ford Mondeo), Alain MENU (Renault Laguna), James THOMPSON (Honda Accord) **DID NOT START** Matt NEAL (Nissan Primera)

SNETTERTON - AUGUST 9-10

QUALIFYING TIMES - ROUND 17

1	Alain MENU	1:08.839
2	Anthony REID	1:08.957
3	James THOMPSON	1:09.057
4	Frank BIELA	1:09.071
5	Jason PLATO	1:09.238
6	Rickard RYDELL	1:09.348
7	Paul RADISICH	1:09.442
8	Patrick WATTS	1:09.449
9	Tim HARVEY	1:09.478
10	John CLELAND	1:09.556
11	Will HOY	1:09.611
12	David LESLIE	1:09.657
13	John BINTCLIFFE	1:09.877
14	Gabriele TARQUINI	1:09.908
15	Derek WARWICK	1:09.920
16	Kelvin BURT	1:09.989
17	Matt NEAL	1:10.190
18	Robb GRAVETT	1:10.583
19	Lee BROOKES	1:10.739
20	Colin GALLIE	1:12.558
21	Jamie WALL	1:12.955
22	Ian HEWARD	1:17.365

RESULTS - ROUND 17   23 LAPS; 44.85 MILES

1	Alain MENU	Renault Laguna	27:12.654	1:10.024
2	James THOMPSON	Honda Accord	27:14.589	1:10.037
3	Frank BIELA	Audi A4 quattro	27:32.838	1:10.849
4	Jason PLATO	Renault Laguna	27:33.378	1:10.251
5	Rickard RYDELL	Volvo S40	27:35.490	1:10.804
6	Paul RADISICH	Ford Mondeo	27:38.865	1:11.148
7	John CLELAND	Vauxhall Vectra	27:40.425	1:11.162
8	Tim HARVEY	Peugeot 406	27:47.398	1:11.174
9	David LESLIE	Nissan Primera	27:47.803	1:11.231
10	Will HOY	Ford Mondeo	27:49.389	1:11.373

11 Derek WARWICK (Vauxhall Vectra) 27:50.193, 12 John BINTCLIFFE (Audi A4 quattro) 27:51.296, 13 Lee BROOKES (Peugeot 406) 28:16.703, 14 Robb GRAVETT (Honda Accord) 22 laps, 15 Colin GALLIE (BMW 320i) 22 laps

NOT CLASSIFIED

Matt NEAL (Nissan Primera), Jamie WALL (Vauxhall Cavalier), Patrick WATTS (Peugeot 406), Kelvin BURT (Volvo S40), Gabriele TARQUINI (Honda Accord), Anthony REID (Nissan Primera) **DID NOT QUALIFY** Ian HEWARD (Vauxhall Cavalier)

QUALIFYING TIMES - ROUND 18

1	Alain MENU	1:09.346
2	Jason PLATO	1:09.585
3	David LESLIE	1:09.675
4	Gabriele TARQUINI	1:09.682
5	Rickard RYDELL	1:09.687
6	James THOMPSON	1:09.701
7	Will HOY	1:09.750
8	Kelvin BURT	1:09.950
9	Patrick WATTS	1:10.026
10	Tim HARVEY	1:10.090
11	Frank BIELA	1:10.196
12	Derek WARWICK	1:10.211
13	Matt NEAL	1:10.387
14	John BINTCLIFFE	1:10.433
15	John CLELAND	1:10.462
16	Lee BROOKES	1:11.300
17	Robb GRAVETT	1:11.424
18	Colin GALLIE	1:12.883
19	Jamie WALL	1:13.555
20	Ian HEWARD	1:18.268
21	Anthony REID	time disallowed
22	Paul RADISICH	time disallowed

RESULTS - ROUND 18   23 LAPS; 44.85 MILES

1	Jason PLATO	Renault Laguna	27:15.149	1:10.002
2	Alain MENU	Renault Laguna	27:15.530	1:09.871
3	Gabriele TARQUINI	Honda Accord	27:15.826	1:10.256
4	James THOMPSON	Honda Accord	27:20.079	1:10.157
5	Rickard RYDELL	Volvo S40	27:23.612	1:10.411
6	David LESLIE	Nissan Primera	27:24.044	1:10.549
7	Will HOY	Ford Mondeo	27:29.977	1:10.609
8	Kelvin BURT	Volvo S40	27:30.928	1:10.502
9	Frank BIELA	Audi A4 quattro	27:31.255	1:10.748
10	Anthony REID	Nissan Primera	27:31.666	1:09.932

11 John BINTCLIFFE (Audi A4 quattro) 27:44.083, 12 Matt NEAL (Nissan Primera) 28:11.834, 13 Robb GRAVETT (Honda Accord) 28:27.330, 14 Colin GALLIE (BMW 320i) 28:29.424, 15 Tim HARVEY (Peugeot 406) 22 laps, 16 John CLELAND (Vauxhall Vectra) 21 laps.

NOT CLASSIFIED

Patrick WATTS (Peugeot 406), Derek WARWICK (Vauxhall Vectra), Paul RADISICH (Ford Mondeo), Lee BROOKES (Peugeot 406) **DID NOT QUALIFY** Ian HEWARD (Vauxhall Cavalier)

THRUXTON - AUGUST 23/25

QUALIFYING TIMES - ROUND 19

1	Rickard RYDELL	1:16.341
2	James THOMPSON	1:16.762
3	John BINTCLIFFE	1:16.811
4	Alain MENU	1:16.859
5	Frank BIELA	1:16.944
6	Gabriele TARQUINI	1:16.962
7	Anthony REID	1:17.219
8	David LESLIE	1:17.487
9	Paul RADISICH	1:17.611
10	John CLELAND	1:17.677
11	Will HOY	1:17.765
12	Tim HARVEY	1:18.009
13	Kelvin BURT	1:18.203
14	Jason PLATO	1:18.307
15	Matt NEAL	1:18.873
16	Lee BROOKES	1:18.940
17	Patrick WATTS	1:19.410
18	Robb GRAVETT	1:19.628
19	Jamie WALL	1:20.097
20	Colin GALLIE	1:21.395
21	Ian HEWARD	1:25.939

RESULTS - ROUND 19   20 LAPS; 47.20 MILES

1	John BINTCLIFFE	Audi A4 quattro	26:30.915	1:18.313
2	Frank BIELA	Audi A4 quattro	26:31.273	1:18.417
3	James THOMPSON	Honda Accord	26:32.687	1:18.384
4	Gabriele TARQUINI	Honda Accord	26:32.883	1:17.876
5	Will HOY	Ford Mondeo	26:46.360	1:18.712
6	Tim HARVEY	Peugeot 406	26:56.822	1:19.024
7	Jason PLATO	Renault Laguna	26:57.222	1:18.735
8	David LESLIE	Nissan Primera	27:03.874	1:19.495
9	Derek WARWICK	Vauxhall Vectra	27:13.048	1:19.894
10	Lee BROOKES	Peugeot 406	27:14.148	1:20.047

11 Matt NEAL (Nissan Primera) 27:15.993, 12 Patrick WATTS (Peugeot 406) 27:20.851, 13 Anthony REID (Nissan Primera) 27:40.699, 14 Paul RADISICH (Ford Mondeo) 27:45.928, 15 Colin GALLIE (BMW 320i) 27:50.127, 16 Robb GRAVETT (Honda Accord) 19 laps, 17 Alain MENU (Renault Laguna) 19 laps, 18 Jamie WALL (Vauxhall Cavalier) 19 laps, 19 John CLELAND (Vauxhall Vectra) 19 laps.

NOT CLASSIFIED Rickard RYDELL (Volvo S40), Kelvin BURT (Volvo S40). **DID NOT QUALIFY** Ian HEWARD (Vauxhall Cavalier)

QUALIFYING TIMES - ROUND 20

1	James THOMPSON	1:16.392
2	Frank BIELA	1:16.413
3	Alain MENU	1:16.452
4	Rickard RYDELL	1:16.526
5	Gabriele TARQUINI	1:16.700
6	Anthony REID	1:17.023
7	John BINTCLIFFE	1:17.266
8	Jason PLATO	1:17.394
9	Paul RADISICH	1:17.601
10	Derek WARWICK	1:17.736
11	Kelvin BURT	1:17.846
12	Will HOY	1:17.983
13	John CLELAND	1:18.075
14	Tim HARVEY	1:18.279
15	Patrick WATTS	1:18.337
16	Matt NEAL	1:18.454
17	Lee BROOKES	1:18.698
18	Robb GRAVETT	1:19.445
19	Jamie WALL	1:20.223
20	Colin GALLIE	1:20.722
21	Ian HEWARD	1:27.190

RESULTS - ROUND 20   20 LAPS; 47.20 MILES

1	Frank BIELA	Audi A4 quattro	26:25.410	1:17.729
2	Alain MENU	Renault Laguna	26:27.804	1:17.915
3	James THOMPSON	Honda Accord	26:37.083	1:17.875
4	Gabriele TARQUINI	Honda Accord	26:39.647	1:18.114
5	John BINTCLIFFE	Audi A4 quattro	26:45.246	1:18.089
6	Jason PLATO	Renault Laguna	26:49.215	1:18.315
7	Rickard RYDELL	Volvo S40	26:49.255	1:18.280
8	Derek WARWICK	Vauxhall Vectra	26:50.657	1:18.471
9	Will HOY	Ford Mondeo	26:55.223	1:18.274
10	David LESLIE	Nissan Primera	26:55.508	1:18.334

11 John CLELAND (Vauxhall Vectra) 26:55.576 , 12 Paul RADISICH (Ford Mondeo) 27:03.001, 13 Tim HARVEY (Peugeot 406) 27:16.883, 14 Lee BROOKES (Peugeot 406) 27:17.814, 15 Jamie WALL (Vauxhall Cavalier) 27:33.737, 16 Kelvin BURT (Volvo S40) 19 laps, 17 Colin GALLIE (BMW 320i) 19 laps.

NOT CLASSIFIED

Anthony REID (Nissan Primera), Robb GRAVETT (Honda Accord), Patrick WATTS (Peugeot 406), Matt NEAL (Nissan Primera). **DID NOT QUALIFY** Ian HEWARD (Vauxhall Cavalier)

BRANDS HATCH - SEPTEMBER 6-7

QUALIFYING TIMES - ROUND 21

1	Frank BIELA	44.619
2	Gabriele TARQUINI	44.677
3	John BINTCLIFFE	44.692
4	Alain MENU	44.699
5	Jason PLATO	44.746
6	David LESLIE	44.769
7	James THOMPSON	44.792
8	Rickard RYDELL	44.802
9	Paul RADISICH	44.909
10	Patrick WATTS	44.999
11	Will HOY	45.016
12	John CLELAND	45.105
13	Kelvin BURT	45.117
14	Derek WARWICK	45.151
15	Tim HARVEY	45.196
16	Matt NEAL	45.215
17	Lee BROOKES	45.777
18	Robb GRAVETT	45.838
19	Anthony REID	46.030
20	Colin GALLIE	46.676
21	Jamie WALL	47.030

RESULTS - ROUND 21   38 LAPS; 45.60 MILES

1	Frank BIELA	Audi A4 quattro	29:12.007	45.178
2	Jason PLATO	Renault Laguna	29:13.879	45.162
3	Alain MENU	Renault Laguna	29:14.470	45.152
4	John BINTCLIFFE	Audi A4 quattro	29:22.022	45.567
5	Tim HARVEY	Peugeot 406	29:25.944	45.629
6	David LESLIE	Nissan Primera	29:27.257	45.180
7	Will HOY	Ford Mondeo	29:27.563	45.679
8	Patrick WATTS	Peugeot 406	29:44.916	46.006
9	Lee BROOKES	Peugeot 406	29:56.769	46.027
10	Robb GRAVETT	Honda Accord	37 laps	46.317

11 Colin GALLIE (BMW 320i) 37 laps, 12 Jamie WALL (Vauxhall Cavalier) 35 laps, John CLELAND (Vauxhall Vectra) 34 laps, 14 Kelvin BURT (Volvo S40) 33 laps, 15 Rickard RYDELL (Volvo S40) 33 laps.

NOT CLASSIFIED Anthony REID (Nissan Primera), Gabriele TARQUINI (Honda Accord), James THOMPSON (Honda Accord), Paul RADISICH (Ford Mondeo), Matt NEAL (Nissan Primera), Derek WARWICK (Vauxhall Vectra)

UNISYS

QUALIFYING TIMES - ROUND 22

1	Anthony REID	44.674
2	James THOMPSON	44.831
3	Rickard RYDELL	44.861
4	Paul RADISICH	45.072
5	Alain MENU	45.152
6	Jason PLATO	45.162
7	Frank BIELA	45.178
8	David LESLIE	45.180
9	Kelvin BURT	45.203
10	Gabriele TARQUINI	45.216
11	John CLELAND	45.398
11	John BINTCLIFFE	45.567
12	Tim HARVEY	45.629
13	Will HOY	45.679
14	Patrick WATTS	46.006
15	Lee BROOKES	46.027
16	Robb GRAVETT	46.317
17	Matt NEAL	46.381
18	Derek WARWICK	46.685
19	Colin GALLIE	46.999
20	Jamie WALL	47.181

RESULTS - ROUND 22
38 LAPS; 45.60 MILES

1	Rickard RYDELL	Volvo S40	29:04.698	45.223
2	Anthony REID	Nissan Primera	29:08.260	45.231
3	Alain MENU	Renault Laguna	29:12.907	45.552
4	Paul RADISICH	Ford Mondeo	29:15.153	45.484
5	Frank BIELA	Audi A4 quattro	29:15.589	45.349
6	Kelvin BURT	Volvo S40	29:16.028	
7				45.449
8	Gabriele TARQUINI	Honda Accord	29:16.380	45.519
9	David LESLIE	Nissan Primera	29:26.798	45.641
10	Tim HARVEY	Peugeot 406	29:28.072	45.733
	Patrick WATTS	Peugeot 406	29:32.915	45.821

11 John BINTCLIFFE (Audi A4 quattro) 29:34.356, 12 John CLELAND (Vauxhall Vectra) 29:44.791, 13 Lee BROOKES (Peugeot 406) 29:47.405, 14 Robb GRAVETT (Honda Accord) 37 laps, 15 Colin GALLIE (BMW 320i) 37 laps, 16 Matt NEAL (Nissan Primera) 37 laps, 17 Jamie WALL (Vauxhall Cavalier) 37 laps.

NOT CLASSIFIED
Will HOY (Ford Mondeo), Jason PLATO (Renault Laguna), James THOMPSON (Honda Accord), Derek WARWICK (Vauxhall Vectra)

SILVERSTONE - SEPTEMBER 20-21

QUALIFYING TIMES - ROUND 23

1	Jason PLATO	1:23.397
2	Gabriele TARQUINI	1:23.508
3	Alain MENU	1:23.646
4	Anthony REID	1:23.689
5	James THOMPSON	1:23.707
6	David LESLIE	1:24.218
7	Kelvin BURT	1:24.227
8	Patrick WATTS	1:24.309
9	Rickard RYDELL	1:24.315
10	Paul RADISICH	1:24.417
11	John BINTCLIFFE	1:24.628
12	Frank BIELA	1:24.629
13	Will HOY	1:24.776
14	Derek WARWICK	1:24.792
15	Tim HARVEY	1:24.859
16	John CLELAND	1:24.946
17	Matt NEAL	1:25.416
18	Lee BROOKES	1:25.759
19	Robb GRAVETT	1:26.003
20	Colin GALLIE	1:27.728
21	Jamie WALL	1:27.963
22	Ian HEWARD	1:33.257

RESULTS - ROUND 23
17 LAPS; 42.84 MILES

1	Alain MENU	Renault Laguna	24:13.272	1:24.406
2	Anthony REID	Nissan Primera	24:15.578	1:24.351
3	Jason PLATO	Renault Laguna	24:18.971	1:24.439
4	Gabriele TARQUINI	Honda Accord	24:23.236	1:24.713
5	Kelvin BURT	Volvo S40	24:26.067	1:24.729
6	David LESLIE	Nissan Primera	24:26.685	1:25.070
7	James THOMPSON	Honda Accord	24:27.996	1:24.779
8	Frank BIELA	Audi A4 quattro	24:32.270	1:25.354
9	Patrick WATTS	Peugeot 406	24:39.528	1:25.396
10	Paul RADISICH	Ford Mondeo	24:39.842	1:25.386

11. John BINTCLIFFE (Audi A4 quattro) 24:40.262, 12. John CLELAND (Vauxhall Vectra) 24:40.719, 13. Tim HARVEY (Peugeot 406) 24:41.263, 14. Matt NEAL (Nissan Primera) 24:49.377, 15. Lee BROOKES (Peugeot 406) 24:49.761, 16 Robb GRAVETT (Honda Accord) 25:15.418, 17. Colin GALLIE (BMW 320i) 25:17.462, 18. Rickard RYDELL (Volvo S40) 25:38.105, 19. Jamie WALL (Vauxhall Cavalier) 15 laps

NOT CLASSIFIED Derek WARWICK (Vauxhall Vectra), Will HOY (Ford Mondeo) **DID NOT QUALIFY** Ian HEWARD (Vauxhall Cavalier)

QUALIFYING TIMES - ROUND 24

1	Alain MENU	1:23.226
2	Jason PLATO	1:23.387
3	James THOMPSON	1:23.535
4	Anthony REID	1:23.722
5	Gabriele TARQUINI	1:23.974
6	Frank BIELA	1:24.063
7	Paul RADISICH	1:24.088
8	David LESLIE	1:24.100
9	Rickard RYDELL	1:24.118
10	Kelvin BURT	1:24.235
11	Will HOY	1:24.345
12	Patrick WATTS	1:24.412
13	Tim HARVEY	1:24.435
14	John BINTCLIFFE	1:24.474
15	Derek WARWICK	1:24.523
16	John CLELAND	1:24.799
17	Lee BROOKES	1:25.040
18	Matt NEAL	1:25.079
19	Robb GRAVETT	1:25.497
20	Colin GALLIE	1:27.508
21	Jamie WALL	1:27.726
22	Ian HEWARD	1:31.942

RESULTS - ROUND 24
20 LAPS; 50.40 MILES

1	Jason PLATO	Renault Laguna	28:30.311	1:24.472
2	Alain MENU	Renault Laguna	28:30.560	1:24.407
3	Gabriele TARQUINI	Honda Accord	28:41.777	1:25.000
4	James THOMPSON	Honda Accord	28:49.546	1:24.743
5	Paul RADISICH	Ford Mondeo	28:52.337	1:25.039
6	David LESLIE	Nissan Primera	28:52.659	1:25.213
7	Rickard RYDELL	Volvo S40	28:53.116	1:24.994
8	Kelvin BURT	Volvo S40	28:53.318	1:24.963
9	Patrick WATTS	Peugeot 406	28:56.829	1:25.585
10	Will HOY	Ford Mondeo	29:05.143	1:25.513

11. John CLELAND (Vauxhall Vectra) 29:06.248, 12. Matt NEAL (Nissan Primera) 29:13.194, 13. Colin GALLIE (BMW 320i) 29:43.627, 14 29 Robb GRAVETT (Honda Accord) 29:58.815, 15. Frank BIELA (Audi A4 quattro) 19 laps, 16 Lee BROOKES (Peugeot 406) 19 laps, 17. Jamie WALL (Vauxhall Cavalier) 19 laps.

NOT CLASSIFIED
Anthony REID (Nissan Primera), Derek WARWICK (Vauxhall Vectra), John BINTCLIFFE (Audi A4 quattro), Tim HARVEY (Peugeot 406). **DID NOT QUALIFY** Ian HEWARD (Vauxhall Cavalier)

FINAL CHAMPIONSHIP POINTS

DRIVERS

1	Alain MENU	Renault Laguna	281
2	Frank BIELA	Audi A4 quattro	171
3	Jason PLATO	Renault Laguna	170
4	Rickard RYDELL	Volvo S40	137
5	James THOMPSON	Honda Accord	132
6	Gabriele TARQUINI	Honda Accord	130
7	John BINTCLIFFE	Audi A4 quattro	119
8	David LESLIE	Nissan Primera	87
9	Tim HARVEY	Peugeot 406	66
10	Kelvin BURT	Volvo S40	60
11	Anthony REID	Nissan Primera	56
12	John CLELAND	Vauxhall Vectra	44
13	Paul RADISICH	Ford Mondeo	41
14	Derek WARWICK	Vauxhall Vectra	33
15	Will HOY	Ford Mondeo	27
16	Patrick WATTS	Peugeot 406	26
17	Lee BROOKES	Peugeot 406	5
18	Robb GRAVETT	Honda Accord	3
19	Colin GALLIE	BMW 320i	2

MANUFACTURERS

1	Renault	278
2	Audi	210
3	Honda	209
4	Volvo	191
5	Nissan	155
6	Peugeot	118
7	Ford	113
8	Vauxhall	106

TEAMS

1	Williams Renault Dealer Racing	422
2	Audi Sport UK	283
3	Team Honda Sport	254
4	Volvo S40 Racing	191
5	Vodafone Nissan Racing	142
6	Esso Ultron Team Peugeot	92
7	Vauxhall Sport	77
8	Team Mondeo	62
9	Brookes Motorsport	5
10	Graham Hathaway Racing	3
11	Pyramid Motorsport	2

TOTAL CUP FOR INDEPENDENTS

1	Robb GRAVETT	Honda Accord	236
2	Lee BROOKES	Peugeot 406	225
3	Colin GALLIE	BMW 320i	225
4	Jamie WALL	Vauxhall Cavalier	168
5	Matt Neal	Ford Mondeo/Nissan Primera	166
6	Ian HEWARD	Vauxhall Cavalier	6

PURE SPEED...

RAW POWER...

SHEER EXCITEMENT...

THAT'S

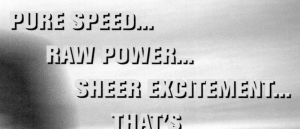

Autosport

International

INCORPORATING THE RACING CAR SHOW

January 9-11th 1998

NEC BIRMINGHAM

GO FOR IT!

The world's Number 1 Racing Car Show gives tribute to the world's Number 1 Racing driver.

In association with the Ayrton Senna Foundation see the cars, trophies and memorablia surrounding the driving legend.*

It's got everything! From the top cars and the latest racing equipment to the top drivers and the leading experts. From F1 and Touring Cars to Rallying and Karting. But for that ultimate thrill, step this way into the Live Action Arena. And you'll be blown away by the wildest display of indoor motorsport theatre! Go for it! And book now for the show of your life.

SAVE £'S AND BEAT THE QUEUES BY CALLING THE TICKET HOTLINE

0121 767 4747

Admission to the LIve Action Arena is only possible via the main show. No public visitors will be permitted entry on Trade Day **Thursday 8th January 1998**

ANOTHER LEADING EVENT PRESENTED BY

HAYMARKET EXHIBITIONS LIMITED
55 NORTH WHARF ROAD, LONDON W2 1LA TELEPHONE: 0171 402 2555 FAX: 0171 402 0920

Indicate the number of tickets you require in the box

Autosport International Show entry	£11.00	☐
Concessions for over 65's and under 15's	£8.00	☐
Live Action Arena seat through Pole Position pre-registration	£5.00	☐
(Admission on the day £8.00)		
Total cheque/postal order value	£ _____	

Please make cheques payable to NEC Box Office

★ Extra admission fee applies

Which day do you wish to attend

☐ **9th Fri** ☐ **10th Sat** ☐ **11th Sun**

If you are booking the LIve Action Arena which performance do you wish to attend?

☐ **11.00am** ☐ **12.30pm** ☐ **2.15pm** ☐ **3.45pm**

If you do not wish to receive other literature please tick box.☐

Admission to the LIve Action Arena is only possible via the main show. No public visitors will be permitted entry on Trade Day **Thursday 8th January 1998**

NAME _____

ADDRESS _____

_____

_____

POSTCODE _____

TEL _____

Return to: Autosport International, NEC Box Office, B40 1NT

aeo Member
Association of Exhibition Organisers

Who won what?

Touring car racing is booming worldwide, with Super Touring the most popular formula, run from Australia to Europe to South America. Here's how the main protagonists, in Super Touring and other classes, fared

The German Super Touring Cup received the best works support of any of the overseas Super Touring series, and Frenchman Laurent Aiello proved the dominant force for Peugeot, winning 11 of the 20 races he contested. However, BMW's Joachim Winkelhock pushed him all the way to the final round where a pair of wins sealed it for Aiello

AUSTRALIAN SUPER TOURING CHAMPIONSHIP

MAY 4 — LAKESIDE
ROUNDS 1 & 2

1	Paul Morris	BMW 320i
2	Geoff Brabham	BMW 320i
3	Jim Richards	Volvo 850
4	Cameron McLean	Opel Vectra
5	Wayne Wakefield	BMW 318i
6	Justin Matthews	BMW 318i

1	Paul Morris	BMW 320i
2	Geoff Brabham	BMW 320i
3	Jim Richards	Volvo 850
4	Brad Jones	Audi A4
5	Cameron McConville	Audi A4
6	Cameron McLean	Opel Vectra

JUNE 1 — PHILLIP ISLAND
ROUNDS 3 & 4

1	Paul Morris	BMW 320i
2	Cameron McConville	Audi A4
3	Steven Richards	Nissan Primera
4	Cameron McLean	Opel Vectra
5	Geoff Brabham	BMW 320i
6	Justin Matthews	BMW 318i

1	Geoff Brabham	BMW 320i
2	Paul Morris	BMW 320i
3	Brad Jones	Audi A4
4	Cameron McConville	Audi A4
5	Jim Richards	Volvo 850
6	Steven Richards	Nissan Primera

JUNE 22 — CALDER PARK
ROUNDS 5 & 6

1	Brad Jones	Audi A4
2	Geoff Brabham	BMW 320i
3	Cameron McConville	Audi A4
4	Jim Richards	Volvo 850
5	Cameron McLean	Opel Vectra
6	Robert Tweedie	Holden Vectra

1	Geoff Brabham	BMW 320i
2	Paul Morris	BMW 320i
3	Cameron McConville	Audi A4
4	Brad Jones	Audi A4
5	Jim Richards	Volvo 850
6	Steven Richards	Nissan Primera

JULY 20 — AMAROO PARK
ROUNDS 7 & 8

1	Brad Jones	Audi A4
2	Paul Morris	BMW 320i
3	Cameron McConville	Audi A4
4	Geoff Brabham	BMW 320i
5	Jim Richards	Volvo 850
6	Steven Richards	Nissan Primera

1	Brad Jones	Audi A4
2	Cameron McConville	Audi A4
3	Geoff Brabham	BMW 320i
4	Paul Morris	BMW 320i
5	Jim Richards	Volvo 850
6	Cameron McLean	Opel Vectra

AUGUST 10 — WINTON
ROUNDS 9 & 10

1	Cameron McConville	Audi A4
2	Paul Morris	BMW 320i
3	Brad Jones	Audi A4
4	Jim Richards	Volvo 850
5	Cameron McLean	Opel Vectra
6	Neal Bates	Toyota Camry

1	Paul Morris	BMW 320i
2	Cameron McConville	Audi A4
3	Geoff Brabham	BMW 320i
4	Jim Richards	Volvo 850
5	Steven Richards	Nissan Primera
6	Brad Jones	Audi A4

AUGUST 24 — MALLALA
ROUNDS 11 & 12

1	Brad Jones	Audi A4
2	Jim Richards	Volvo 850
3	Cameron McConville	Audi A4
4	Cameron McLean	Opel Vectra
5	Neal Bates	Toyota Camry
6	Paul Morris	BMW 320i

1	Cameron McConville	Audi A4
2	Geoff Brabham	BMW 320i
3	Paul Morris	BMW 320i
4	Brad Jones	Audi A4
5	Jim Richards	Volvo 850
6	Cameron McLean	Opel Vectra

OCTOBER 26 — LAKESIDE
ROUNDS 13 & 14

1	Paul Morris	BMW 320i
2	Geoff Brabham	BMW 320i
3	Craig Baird	BMW 320i
4	Cameron McConville	Audi A4
5	Jim Richards	Volvo 850
6	Cameron McLean	Opel Vectra

1	Paul Morris	BMW 320i
2	Geoff Brabham	BMW 320i
3	Craig Baird	BMW 320i
4	Jim Richards	Volvo 850
5	Cameron McLean	Opel Vectra
6	Cameron McConville	Audi A4

CHAMPIONSHIP POSITIONS
(with a round to go at Amaroo Park)

1	Paul Morris	167
2	Geoff Brabham	146
3	Cameron McConville	133
4	Brad Jones	114
5	Jim Richards	100
6	Cameron McLean	67

BELGIAN PROCAR CHAMPIONSHIP

APRIL 20 — ZOLDER
ROUNDS 1 & 2

1	Didier de Radigues	BMW 320i
2	Jean-Francois Hemroulle	Audi A4
3	Vincent Radermecker	Peugeot 406
4	Thierry Tassin	Honda Accord

No other Division 1 finishers

1	Didier de Radigues	BMW 320i
2	Jean-Francois Hemroulle	Audi A4
3	Thierry Tassin	Honda Accord

No other Division 1 finishers

MAY 4 — SPA
ROUNDS 3 & 4

1	Didier de Radigues	BMW 320i
2	Vincent Radermecker	Peugeot 406
3	Thierry Tassin	Honda Accord
4	Jean-Francois Hemroulle	Audi A4
5	Vincent Vosse	Ford Mondeo
6	Christophe Dechavanne	Audi 80

1	Jean-Francois Hemroulle	Audi A4
2	Didier de Radigues	BMW 320i
3	Vincent Radermecker	Peugeot 406
4	Christophe Dechavanne	Audi 80
5	Guino Kenis	BMW 318i
6	Philippe Eliard	Alfa 155

MAY 18 — ZOLDER
ROUNDS 5 & 6

1	Jean-Francois Hemroulle	Audi A4
2	Didier de Radigues	BMW 320i
3	Vincent Radermecker	Peugeot 406
4	Christophe Dechavanne	Audi 80
5	Didier Defourny	Ford Mondeo
6	Philippe Eliard	Alfa 155

1	Jean-Francois Hemroulle	Audi A4
2	Didier de Radigues	BMW 320i
3	Vincent Radermecker	Peugeot 406
4	Thierry Tassin	Honda Accord
5	Christophe Dechavanne	Audi 80
6	Guino Kenis	BMW 318i

JUNE 8 — ZANDVOORT
ROUNDS 7 & 8

1	Jean-Francois Hemroulle	Audi A4
2	Didier de Radigues	BMW 320i
3	Vincent Radermecker	Peugeot 406
4	Christophe Dechavanne	Audi 80
5	Didier Defourny	Ford Mondeo
6	No other Division 1 finishers	

1	Vincent Radermecker	Peugeot 406
2	Jean-Francois Hemroulle	Audi A4
3	Didier de Radigues	BMW 320i
4	Didier Defourny	Ford Mondeo
5	Christophe Dechavanne	Audi 80
6	No other Division 1 finishers	

JUNE 22 — SPA
ROUNDS 9 & 10

1	Gabriele Tarquini	Honda Accord
2	Didier de Radigues	BMW 320i
3	Vincent Radermecker	Peugeot 406
4	Jean-Francois Hemroulle	Audi A4

No other Division 1 finishers

1	Terry Moss	Audi A4
2	Giancarlo Fisichella	Peugeot 406
3	Thierry van Dalen	BMW 318i
4	Phillip Verellen	BMW 318i
5	Thierry Tassin	Honda Accord

No other Division 1 finishers

JULY 6 — CHIMAY
ROUNDS 11 & 12

1	Jean-Francois Hemroulle	Audi A4
2	Vincent Radermecker	Peugeot 406
3	Didier de Radigues	BMW 320i
4	Thierry Tassin	Honda Accord
5	Dider Defourny	BMW 320i
6	Christophe Dechavanne	Audi 80

1	Thierry Tassin	Honda Accord
2	Jean-Francois Hemroulle	Audi A4
3	Didier Defourny	BMW 320i
4	Frederic Moreau	BMW 318i
5	Philippe Eliard	Alfa 155
6	Christophe Dechavanne	Audi 80

SEPTEMBER 6 — ZOLDER
ROUNDS 13 & 14

1	Didier de Radigues	BMW 320i
2	Vincent Radermecker	Peugeot 406
3	Jean-Francois Hemroulle	Audi A4
4	Vincent Vosse	Audi A4
5	Christophe Dechavanne	Audi 80
6	Giampiero Simoni	Alfa Romeo 155

1	Didier de Radigues	BMW 320i
2	Jean-Francois Hemroulle	Audi A4
3	Didier Defourny	BMW 320i
4	Vincent Vosse	Audi A4
5	Christophe Dechavanne	Audi 80
6	Frederic Moreau	BMW 318i

SEPTEMBER 28 — SPA
ROUNDS 15 & 16

1	Didier de Radigues	BMW 320i
2	Vincent Radermecker	Peugeot 406
3	Eric Helary	BMW 320i
4	Thierry Tassin	Honda Accord
5	Jean-Francois Hemroulle	Audi A4
6	Vincent Vosse	Audi A4

1	Didier de Radigues	BMW 320i
2	Eric Helary	BMW 320i
3	Vincent Radermecker	Peugeot 406
4	Thierry Tassin	Honda Accord
5	Jean-Francois Hemroulle	Audi A4
6	Didier Defourny	BMW 320i

CHAMPIONSHIP POSITIONS

1	Didier de Radigues	234
2	Jean-Francois Hemroulle	228
3	Vincent Radermecker	175
4	Thierry Tassin	116
5	Christophe Dechavanne	93
6	Didier Defourny	67

GERMAN SUPER TOURING CUP

APRIL 27 — HOCKENHEIM
ROUNDS 1 & 2

1	Laurent Aiello	Peugeot 406
2	Johnny Cecotto	BMW 320i
3	Jorg van Ommen	Peugeot 406
4	Joachim Winkelhock	BMW 320i
5	Kris Nissen	Audi A4
6	Marco Werner	Honda Accord

1 Laurent Aiello — Peugeot 406
2 Joachim Winkelhock — BMW 320i
3 Johnny Cecotto — BMW 320i
4 Jorg van Ommen — Peugeot 406
5 Marco Werner — Honda Accord
6 Kris Nissen — Audi A4

MAY 11 — ZOLDER
ROUNDS 3 & 4
1 Johnny Cecotto — BMW 320i
2 Joachim Winkelhock — BMW 320i
3 Laurent Aiello — Peugeot 406
4 Emanuele Pirro — Audi A4
5 Christian Abt — Audi A4
6 Philipp Peter — Audi A4

1 Johnny Cecotto — BMW 320i
2 Joachim Winkelhock — BMW 320i
3 Laurent Aiello — Peugeot 406
4 Christian Abt — Audi A4
5 Philipp Peter — Audi A4
6 Kris Nissen — Audi A4

MAY 25 — NURBURGRING
ROUNDS 5 & 6
1 Laurent Aiello — Peugeot 406
2 Marco Werner — Honda Accord
3 Johnny Cecotto — BMW 320i
4 Jorg van Ommen — Peugeot 406
5 Altfrid Heger — Honda Accord
6 Uwe Alzen — Opel Vectra

1 Laurent Aiello — Peugeot 406
2 Johnny Cecotto — BMW 320i
3 Marco Werner — Honda Accord
4 Altfrid Heger — Honda Accord
5 Jorg van Ommen — Peugeot 406
6 Emanuele Pirro — Audi A4

JUNE 15 — SACHSENRING
ROUNDS 7 & 8
1 Joachim Winkelhock — BMW 320i
2 Laurent Aiello — Peugeot 406
3 Uwe Alzen — Opel Vectra
4 Emanuele Pirro — Audi A4
5 Jorg van Ommen — Peugeot 406
6 Philipp Peter — Audi A4

1 Joachim Winkelhock — BMW 320i
2 Laurent Aiello — Peugeot 406
3 Uwe Alzen — Opel Vectra
4 Jorg van Ommen — Peugeot 406
5 Johnny Cecotto — BMW 320i
6 Yvan Muller — Audi A4

JUNE 29 — NORISRING
ROUNDS 9 & 10
1 Joachim Winkelhock — BMW 320i
2 Laurent Aiello — Peugeot 406
3 Jorg van Ommen — Peugeot 406
4 Johnny Cecotto — BMW 320i
5 Emanuele Pirro — Audi A4
6 Christian Abt — Audi A4

1 Joachim Winkelhock — BMW 320i
2 Jorg van Ommen — Peugeot 406
3 Emanuele Pirro — Audi A4
4 Kris Nissen — Audi A4
5 Tamara Vidali — Audi A4
6 Roland Asch — Nissan Primera

JULY 13 — WUNSTORF
ROUNDS 11 & 12
1 Laurent Aiello — Peugeot 406
2 Joachim Winkelhock — BMW 320i
3 Uwe Alzen — Opel Vectra
4 Kurt Thiim — Opel Vectra
5 Marco Werner — Honda Accord
6 Jorg van Ommen — Peugeot 406

1 Laurent Aiello — Peugeot 406
2 Uwe Alzen — Opel Vectra
3 Joachim Winkelhock — BMW 320i
4 Kurt Thiim — Opel Vectra
5 Johnny Cecotto — BMW 320i
6 Manuel Reuter — Opel Vectra

AUGUST 10 — ZWEIBRUCKEN
ROUNDS 13 & 14
1 Laurent Aiello — Peugeot 406
2 Joachim Winkelhock — BMW 320i
3 Johnny Cecotto — BMW 320i
4 Emanuele Pirro — Audi A4
5 Philipp Peter — Audi A4
6 Yvan Muller — Audi A4

1 Emanuele Pirro — Audi A4
2 Johnny Cecotto — BMW 320i
3 Philipp Peter — Audi A4
4 Laurent Aiello — Peugeot 406
5 Joachim Winkelhock — BMW 320i
6 Yvan Muller — Audi A4

AUGUST 24 — SALZBURGRING
ROUNDS 15 & 16
1 Laurent Aiello — Peugeot 406
2 Jorg van Ommen — Peugeot 406
3 Uwe Alzen — Opel Vectra
4 Joachim Winkelhock — BMW 320i
5 Michael Bartels — Opel Vectra
6 Yvan Muller — Audi A4

1 Laurent Aiello — Peugeot 406
2 Joachim Winkelhock — BMW 320i
3 Uwe Alzen — Opel Vectra
4 Michael Bartels — Opel Vectra
5 Johnny Cecotto — BMW 320i
6 Yvan Muller — Audi A4

SEPTEMBER 7 — LAHR
ROUNDS 17 & 18
1 Johnny Cecotto — BMW 320i
2 Laurent Aiello — Peugeot 406
3 Uwe Alzen — Opel Vectra
4 Yvan Muller — Audi A4
5 Christian Menzel — BMW 320i
6 Jorg van Ommen — Peugeot 406

1 Joachim Winkelhock — BMW 320i
2 Johnny Cecotto — BMW 320i
3 Uwe Alzen — Opel Vectra
4 Yvan Muller — Audi A4
5 Kurt Thiim — Opel Vectra
6 Michael Bartels — Opel Vectra

OCTOBER 5 — NURBURGRING
ROUNDS 19 & 20
1 Laurent Aiello — Peugeot 406
2 Jorg van Ommen — Peugeot 406
3 Joachim Winkelhock — BMW 320i
4 Michael Bartels — Opel Vectra
5 Johnny Cecotto — BMW 320i
6 Uwe Alzen — Opel Vectra

1 Laurent Aiello — Peugeot 406
2 Joachim Winkelhock — BMW 320i
3 Johnny Cecotto — BMW 320i
4 Jorg van Ommen — Peugeot 406
5 Michael Bartels — Opel Vectra
6 Yvan Muller — Audi A4

CHAMPIONSHIP POSITIONS
1 Laurent Aiello — 696
2 Joachim Winkelhock — 644
3 Johnny Cecotto — 571
4 Jorg van Ommen — 377
5 Uwe Alzen — 370
6 Emanuele Pirro — 357

ITALIAN SUPER TOURING CHAMPIONSHIP

APRIL 20 — MONZA
ROUNDS 1 & 2
1 Emanuele Naspetti — BMW 320i
2 Rinaldo Capello — Audi A4
3 Karl Wendlinger — Audi A4
4 Gordon de Adamich — Alfa 155
5 Massimo Pigoli — BMW 320i
6 Sandro Sardelli — Opel Vectra

1 Emanuele Naspetti — BMW 320i
2 Roberto Colciago — Honda Accord
3 Fabrizio de Simone — BMW 320i
4 Karl Wendlinger — Audi A4
5 Massimo Pigoli — BMW 320i
6 Moreno Soli — Alfa 155

MAY 4 — MUGELLO
ROUNDS 3 & 4
1 Emanuele Naspetti — BMW 320i
2 Roberto Colciago — Honda Accord
3 Karl Wendlinger — Audi A4
4 Antonio Tamburini — Alfa 155
5 Fabrizio Giovanardi — Alfa 155
6 Gianluca Roda — Opel Vectra

1 Fabrizio Giovanardi — Alfa 155
2 Emanuele Naspetti — BMW 320i
3 Antonio Tamburini — Alfa 155
4 Karl Wendlinger — Audi A4
5 Moreno Soli — Alfa 155
6 Sandro Montani — Alfa 155

MAY 18 — MAGIONE
ROUNDS 5 & 6
1 Emanuele Naspetti — BMW 320i
2 Fabrizio de Simone — BMW 320i
3 Roberto Colciago — Honda Accord
4 Antonio Tamburini — Alfa 155
5 Rinaldo Capello — Audi A4
6 Massimo Pigoli — BMW 320i

1 Emanuele Naspetti — BMW 320i
2 Fabrizio de Simone — BMW 320i
3 Rinaldo Capello — Audi A4
4 Antonio Tamburini — Alfa 155
5 Fabrizio Giovanardi — Alfa 155
6 Massimo Pigoli — BMW 320i

JUNE 8 — IMOLA
ROUNDS 7 & 8
1 Fabrizio Giovanardi — Alfa 155
2 Emanuele Naspetti — BMW 320i
3 Fabrizio de Simone — BMW 320i
4 Rinaldo Capello — Audi A4
5 Roberto Colciago — Honda Accord
6 Karl Wendlinger — Audi A4

1 Emanuele Naspetti — BMW 320i
2 Rinaldo Capello — Audi A4
3 Fabrizio de Simone — BMW 320i
4 Antonio Tamburini — Alfa 155
5 Roberto Colciago — Honda Accord
6 Karl Wendlinger — Audi A4

JUNE 22 — IMOLA
ROUNDS 9 & 10
1 Antonio Tamburini — Alfa 155
2 Emanuele Naspetti — BMW 320i
3 Karl Wendlinger — Audi A4
4 Rinaldo Capello — Audi A4
5 Massimo Pigoli — BMW 320i
6 Sandro Sardelli — Opel Vectra

1 Emanuele Naspetti — BMW 320i
2 Fabrizio Giovanardi — Alfa 155
3 Rinaldo Capello — Audi A4
4 Fabrizio de Simone — BMW 320i
5 Antonio Tamburini — Alfa 155
6 Roberto Colciago — Honda Accord

JULY 6 — BINETTO
ROUNDS 11 & 12
1 Emanuele Naspetti — BMW 320i
2 Rinaldo Capello — Audi A4
3 Karl Wendlinger — Audi A4
4 Fabrizio Giovanardi — Alfa 155
5 Massimo Pigoli — BMW 320i
6 Moreno Soli — Alfa 155

1 Rinaldo Capello — Audi A4
2 Emanuele Naspetti — BMW 320i
3 Karl Wendlinger — Audi A4
4 Fabrizio Giovanardi — Alfa 155
5 Roberto Colciago — Honda Accord
6 Massimo Pigoli — BMW 320i

AUGUST 31 — ENNA-PERGUSA
ROUNDS 13 & 14
1 Fabrizio Giovanardi — Alfa 155
2 Emanuele Naspetti — BMW 320i
3 Roberto Colciago — Honda Accord
4 Karl Wendlinger — Audi A4
5 Rinaldo Capello — Audi A4
6 Massimo Pigoli — BMW 320i

1 Fabrizio Giovanardi — Alfa 155
2 Emanuele Naspetti — BMW 320i
3 Fabrizio de Simone — BMW 320i
4 Roberto Colciago — Honda Accord
5 Karl Wendlinger — Audi A4
6 Antonio Tamburini — Alfa 155

SEPTEMBER 14 — VARANO
ROUNDS 15 & 16
1 Rinaldo Capello — Audi A4
2 Fabrizio Giovanardi — Alfa 155
3 Karl Wendlinger — Audi A4
4 Antonio Tamburini — Alfa 155
5 Emanuele Naspetti — BMW 320i
6 Sandro Sardelli — Opel Vectra

1 Rinaldo Capello — Audi A4
2 Fabrizio Giovanardi — Alfa 155
3 Karl Wendlinger — Audi A4
4 Antonio Tamburini — Alfa 155
5 Fabrizio de Simone — BMW 320i
6 Sandro Sardelli — Opel Vectra

SEPTEMBER 28 — MISANO
ROUNDS 17 & 18
1 Emanuele Naspetti — BMW 320i
2 Fabrizio Giovanardi — Alfa 155
3 Fabrizio de Simone — BMW 320i
4 Antonio Tamburini — Alfa 155
5 Roberto Colciago — Honda Accord
6 Rinaldo Capello — Audi A4

1 Emanuele Naspetti — BMW 320i
2 Fabrizio Giovanardi — Alfa 155
3 Fabrizio de Simone — BMW 320i
4 Roberto Colciago — Honda Accord
5 Karl Wendlinger — Audi A4
6 Antonio Tamburini — Alfa 155

OCTOBER 12 — VALLELUNGA
ROUNDS 19 & 20
1 Fabrizio Giovanardi — Alfa 155
2 Emanuele Naspetti — BMW 320i
3 Fabrizio de Simone — BMW 320i
4 Roberto Colciago — Honda Accord
5 Antonio Tamburini — Alfa 155
6 Rinaldo Capello — Audi A4

1 Fabrizio de Simone — BMW 320i
2 Fabrizio Giovanardi — Alfa 155
3 Emanuele Naspetti — BMW 320i
4 Rinaldo Capello — Audi A4
5 Antonio Tamburini — Alfa 155
6 Karl Wendlinger — Audi A4

CHAMPIONSHIP POSITIONS
1 Emanuele Naspetti — 325
2 Fabrizio Giovanardi — 229
3 Rinaldo Capello — 190
4 Fabrizio de Simone — 157
5 Karl Wendlinger — 156
6 Antonio Tamburini — 140

ALL-JAPAN TOURING CAR CHAMPIONSHIP

MAY 11 — TI CIRCUIT
ROUNDS 1 & 2
1 Takuya Kurosawa — Honda Accord
2 Osamu Nakako — Honda Accord
3 Ryo Michigami — Honda Accord
4 Satoshi Motoyama — Nissan Primera
5 Masami Kageyama — Toyota Exiv
6 Kazuyoshi Hoshino — Nissan Primera

1 Osamu Nakako — Honda Accord
2 Satoshi Motoyama — Nissan Primera
3 Ryo Michigami — Honda Accord
4 Takuya Kurosawa — Honda Accord
5 Hironori Takeuchi — Toyota Chaser
6 Masami Kageyama — Toyota Exiv

MAY 25 — SUGO
ROUNDS 3 & 4
1 Michael Krumm — Toyota Exiv
2 Kazuyoshi Hoshino — Nissan Primera
3 Satoshi Motoyama — Nissan Primera
4 Akira Iida — Opel Vectra
5 Takuya Kurosawa — Honda Accord
6 Hironori Takeuchi — Toyota Chaser

1 Kazuyoshi Hoshino — Nissan Primera
2 Juan Manuel Silva — Toyota Exiv
3 Satoshi Motoyama — Nissan Primera
4 Hideki Okada — Honda Accord
5 Akira Iida — Opel Vectra
6 Takuya Kurosawa — Honda Accord

JUNE 8 — SUZUKA
ROUNDS 5 & 6
1 Takuya Kurosawa — Honda Accord
2 Kazuyoshi Hoshino — Nissan Primera
3 Masami Kageyama — Toyota Exiv
4 Osamu Nakako — Honda Accord
5 Ryo Michigami — Honda Accord
6 Akira Iida — Opel Vectra

1 Satoshi Motoyama — Nissan Primera
2 Takuya Kurosawa — Honda Accord
3 Masami Kageyama — Toyota Exiv
4 Ryo Michigami — Honda Accord
5 Osamu Nakako — Honda Accord
6 Kazuyoshi Hoshino — Nissan Primera

JULY 13 — MINE
ROUNDS 7 & 8
1 Osamu Nakako — Honda Accord
2 Ryo Michigami — Honda Accord
3 Katsutomo Kaneishi — Toyota Exiv
4 Kazuyoshi Hoshino — Nissan Primera
5 Masami Kageyama — Toyota Exiv
6 Michael Krumm — Toyota Exiv

1 Osamu Nakako — Honda Accord
2 Ryo Michigami — Honda Accord
3 Satoshi Motoyama — Nissan Primera
4 Michael Krumm — Toyota Exiv
5 Hideki Okada — Honda Accord
6 Takuya Kurosawa — Honda Accord

SEPTEMBER 7 — SENDAI
ROUNDS 9 & 10
1 Satoshi Motoyama — Nissan Primera
2 Kazuyoshi Hoshino — Nissan Primera
3 Akira Iida — Opel Vectra
4 Osamu Nakako — Honda Accord
5 Masami Kageyama — Toyota Exiv
6 Juan Manuel Silva — Toyota Exiv

1 Akira Iida — Opel Vectra
2 Ryo Michigami — Honda Accord
3 Masanori Sekiya — Toyota Exiv
4 Hironori Takeuchi — Toyota Chaser
5 Katsutomo Kaneishi — Toyota Exiv
6 Takuya Kurosawa — Honda Accord

SEPTEMBER 21 — TOKACHI
ROUNDS 11 & 12
1 Takuya Kurosawa — Honda Accord
2 Satoshi Motoyama — Nissan Primera
3 Kazuyoshi Hoshino — Nissan Primera
4 Katsutomo Kaneishi — Toyota Exiv
5 Ryo Michigami — Honda Accord
6 Masami Kageyama — Toyota Exiv

1 Takuya Kurosawa — Honda Accord
2 Osamu Nakako — Honda Accord
3 Ryo Michigami — Honda Accord
4 Satoshi Motoyama — Nissan Primera
5 Katsutomo Kaneishi — Toyota Exiv
6 Masanori Sekiya — Toyota Chaser

CHAMPIONSHIP POSITIONS
(with one round to go at Fuji)
1 Takuya Kurosawa — 100
2 Satoshi Motoyama — 95
3 Osamu Nakako — 93

NORTH AMERICAN SUPER TOURING CHAMPIONSHIP

APRIL 13 — LONG BEACH
ROUNDS 1 & 2
1 Neil Crompton — Honda Accord
2 Dominic Dobson — Dodge Stratus
3 Randy Pobst — BMW 320i
4 David Donohue — Dodge Stratus
5 Bob Schader — Mazda Xedos
6 Desire Wilson — Mazda Xedos

1 Neil Crompton — Honda Accord
2 Randy Pobst — BMW 320i
3 Dominic Dobson — Dodge Stratus
4 David Donohue — Dodge Stratus
5 David Welch — Ford Mondeo
6 Darren Law — BMW 320i

AR3

PA, AUDIO & VISUAL SERVICES FOR ALL
APPLICATIONS - CONFERENCES, EVENTS,
PRODUCTIONS, LAUNCHES, SPORTING FIXTURES
AND PERMANENT VENUES.

AR3

EVENT TECHNICAL SERVICES

EVENT TECHNICAL SERVICES FROM THE
PROVISION OF A SINGLE GENERATOR TO A
COMPLETE PACKAGE FOR A CORPORATE
HOSPITALITY VILLAGE.

race RADIO

SPECIAL EVENT MOBILE RADIO STUDIOS
COMPLETE WITH AM/FM TRANSMISSION.

AVAILABLE FROM STOCK

INDOOR PA SYSTEMS

OUTDOOR PA SYSTEMS

TWO WAY RADIO

RADIO MICROPHONES

COMMENTARY VEHICLES

DOUBLE DECKER CONTROL UNITS

HOSPITALITY TV

VIDEO SYSTEMS

SATELLITE SYSTEMS

VIDEO AND FILM PROJECTION

VIDEO RECORDING

VIDEO WALL

AUDIO VISUAL PRODUCTION

EVACUATION PA SYSTEM

CHANDELIERS

DECORATIVE LIGHTING

UTILITY LIGHTING

BROADCAST CAMERA FACILITIES

TV AND VIDEO PRODUCTION

DRIVE-IN VIDEO STUDIO

IN-HOUSE EDITING

RESEARCH AND SCRIPT WRITING

MEETING PRESENTATION

CONFERENCE PRESENTATION

EVENT RADIO STATION

MOBILE RADIO VEHICLES

SUPERSILENT GENERATORS

MODULAR POWER DISTRIBUTION

COOLING/HEATING EQUIPMENT

FIRE ALARMS

FIRE EXTINGUISHERS

TIMING EQUIPMENT

ENGINEERS AND TECHNICIANS

PAT TESTING

16TH EDITION TESTING

THE STUDIO,

OVERTHORPE ROAD,

BANBURY,

OXON OX16 8SX

TEL: 01295 262000

FAX: 01295 271386

ON SITE SILVERSTONE

TEL: 01327 858269

ON SITE NAC STONELEIGH

TEL: 01203 417733

It's a downer when you don't know the full story...

AUTOSPORT
Puts you in the picture

THE WORLD'S BEST MOTORSPORT WEEKLY. ON SALE EVERY THURSDAY

MAY 18 — SAVANNAH
ROUNDS 3 & 4
1 Peter Cunningham — Honda Accord
2 David Donohue — Dodge Stratus
3 Neil Crompton — Honda Accord
4 Dominic Dobson — Dodge Stratus
5 Darren Law — BMW 320i
6 Randy Pobst — BMW 320i

1 Peter Cunningham — Honda Accord
2 Neil Crompton — Honda Accord
3 David Donohue — Dodge Stratus
4 Dominic Dobson — Dodge Stratus
5 Darren Law — BMW 320i
6 Forrest Granlund — Honda Accord

JUNE 8 — DETROIT
ROUNDS 5 & 6
1 David Donohue — Dodge Stratus
2 Dominic Dobson — Dodge Stratus
3 Neil Crompton — Honda Accord
4 Peter Cunningham — Honda Accord
5 David Welch — Ford Mondeo
6 Walt Puckett — Mazda Xedos

1 Dominic Dobson — Dodge Stratus
2 David Welch — Ford Mondeo
3 Bob Schader — Mazda Xedos
4 Forrest Granlund — Honda Accord
5 David Welch — Dodge Stratus
No other finishers

JUNE 22 — PORTLAND
ROUNDS 7 & 8
1 David Donohue — Dodge Stratus
2 Peter Cunningham — Honda Accord
3 Randy Pobst — BMW 320i
4 Darren Law — BMW 320i
5 Tom Finnelly — BMW 320i
6 Dominic Dobson — Dodge Stratus

1 Peter Cunningham — Honda Accord
2 Rod Millen — Toyota Camry
3 Darren Law — BMW 320i
4 Bob Schader — Mazda Xedos
5 Tom Finelly — BMW 320i
6 Randy Pobst — BMW 320i

JULY 13 — CLEVELAND
ROUNDS 9 & 10
1 David Donohue — Dodge Stratus
2 Randy Pobst — BMW 320i
3 Peter Cunningham — Honda Accord
4 Forrest Granlund — Honda Accord
5 Neil Crompton — Honda Accord
6 Bob Schader — Mazda Xedos

1 Peter Cunningham — Honda Accord
2 Neil Crompton — Honda Accord
3 Dominic Dobson — Dodge Stratus
4 Randy Pobst — BMW 320i
5 Darren Law — BMW 320i
6 Forrest Granlund — Honda Accord

JULY 20 — TORONTO
ROUNDS 11 & 12
1 Dominic Dobson — Dodge Stratus
2 Neil Crompton — Honda Accord
3 Peter Cunningham — Honda Accord
4 David Donohue — Dodge Stratus
5 Darren Law — BMW 320i
6 David Welch — Ford Mondeo

1 Neil Crompton — Honda Accord
2 Dominic Dobson — Dodge Stratus
3 Peter Cunningham — Honda Accord
4 David Donohue — Dodge Stratus
5 David Welch — Ford Mondeo
6 Darren Law — BMW 320i

AUGUST 9 — MID-OHIO
ROUNDS 13 & 14
1 David Donohue — Dodge Stratus
2 Neil Crompton — Honda Accord
3 Peter Cunningham — Honda Accord
4 Dominic Dobson — Dodge Stratus
5 Darren Law — BMW 320i
6 Forrest Granlund — Honda Accord

1 David Donohue — Dodge Stratus
2 Peter Cunningham — Honda Accord
3 Neil Crompton — Honda Accord
4 Forrest Granlund — Honda Accord
5 David Welch — Ford Mondeo
6 Darren Law — BMW 320i

AUGUST 31 — VANCOUVER
ROUNDS 15 & 16
1 Neil Crompton — Honda Accord
2 David Donohue — Dodge Stratus
3 Dominic Dobson — Dodge Stratus
4 Peter Cunningham — Honda Accord
5 David Welch — Ford Mondeo
6 Randy Pobst — BMW 320i

1 Neil Crompton — Honda Accord
2 Randy Pobst — BMW 320i
3 Peter Cunningham — Honda Accord
4 David Welch — Ford Mondeo
5 David Donohue — Dodge Stratus
6 Bob Schader — Mazda Xedos

SEPTEMBER 7 — LAGUNA SECA
ROUNDS 17 & 18
1 Neil Crompton — Honda Accord
2 Peter Cunningham — Honda Accord
3 David Donohue — Dodge Stratus
4 Dominic Dobson — Dodge Stratus
5 Randy Pobst — BMW 320i
6 David Welch — Ford Mondeo

1 Neil Crompton — Honda Accord
2 Peter Cunningham — Honda Accord
3 David Donohue — Dodge Stratus
4 Randy Pobst — BMW 320i
5 David Welch — Ford Mondeo
6 Dominic Dobson — Dodge Stratus

CHAMPIONSHIP POSITIONS
1 David Donohue — 304
2 Peter Cunningham — 282
3 Neil Crompton — 280
4 Dominic Dobson — 230
5 Randy Pobst — 188
6 Bob Schader — 185

SOUTH AMERICAN SUPER TOURING CHAMPIONSHIP

JUNE 1 — BUENOS AIRES
ROUND 1
1 Oscar Larrauri — BMW 320i
2 Osvaldo Lopez — Alfa 155
3 Jose Luis di Palma — Chevrolet Vectra
4 Patricio Spinella — BMW 320i
5 Javier Balzano — Chevrolet Vectra
6 Oscar Fineschi — Toyota Corona

JUNE 22 — CURITIBA
ROUND 2
1 Patricio Spinella — BMW 320i
2 Flavio Figueiredo — BMW 320i
3 Patrizio Luis di Palma — Peugeot 406
4 Ricardo Risatti — Ford Mondeo
5 Daniel Marrocchi — Chevrolet Vectra
6 Javier Balzano — Chevrolet Vectra

JULY 6 — RESISTENCIA
ROUND 3
1 Oscar Larrauri — BMW 320i
2 Osvaldo Lopez — Alfa 155
3 Javier Balzano — Chevrolet Vectra
4 Patricio Spinella — BMW 320i
5 Flavio Figueiredo — BMW 320i
6 Daniel Marrocchi — Chevrolet Vectra

AUGUST 3 — ROSARIO
ROUND 4
1 Alejandro Pagani — Chevrolet Vectra
2 Jose Luis di Palma — Chevrolet Vectra
3 Oscar Fineschi — Toyota Corona
4 Javier Balzano — Chevrolet Vectra
5 Oscar Larrauri — BMW 320i
6 Ricardo Risatti — Ford Mondeo

AUGUST 31 — LONDRINA
ROUND 5
1 Osvaldo Lopez — Alfa 155
2 Patricio Spinella — BMW 320i
3 Javier Balzano — Chevrolet Vectra
4 Oscar Fineschi — Toyota Corona
5 Fabian Hermoso — Alfa 155
6 Maurizio Sandro Sala — BMW 320i

SEPTEMBER 14 — BUENOS AIRES
ROUND 6
1 Oscar Fineschi — Toyota Corona
2 Javier Balzano — Chevrolet Vectra
3 Osvaldo Lopez — Alfa 155
4 Oscar Larrauri — BMW 320i
5 Carlos Okulovich — Peugeot 406
6 Patrizio Luis di Palma — Peugeot 406

OCTOBER 19 — BUENOS AIRES
ROUND 7
1 Oscar Larrauri — BMW 320i
2 Jose Luis di Palma — Honda Accord
3 Osvaldo Lopez — Alfa 155
4 Oscar Fineschi — Toyota Corona
5 Patrizio Luis di Palma — Peugeot 406
6 Emiliano Spataro — BMW 320i

CHAMPIONSHIP POSITIONS
(With three rounds to go at Taruma, Interlagos & Buenos Aires)
1 Oscar Larrauri — 80
2 Osvaldo Lopez — 77
3 Oscar Fineschi — 67
4 Javier Balzano — 63
5 Patricio Spinella — 60
6 Jose Luis di Palma — 47

SWEDISH SUPER TOURING CHAMPIONSHIP

MAY 4 — MANTORP PARK
ROUNDS 1 & 2
1 Mattias Ekstrom — Volvo 850
2 Jan Brunstedt — Opel Vectra
3 Stig Blomqvist — Ford Mondeo
4 Kari Makinen — Opel Vectra
5 Anders Soderberg — Ford Mondeo
6 Trygve Enger — BMW 320i

1 Mattias Ekstrom — Volvo 850
2 Kari Makinen — Opel Vectra
3 Georg Bakajev — BMW 320i
4 Elisabeth Nilsson — Ford Mondeo
5 Niklas Danielsson — BMW M3
6 No other finishers

MAY 25 — MANTORP PARK
ROUNDS 3 & 4
1 Jan Nilsson — Volvo 850
2 Thomas Johansson — BMW 320i
3 'Peggen' Andersson — BMW 320i
4 Stig Blomqvist — Ford Mondeo
5 Ulrik Gustavsson — Alfa 155
6 Anders Soderberg — Ford Mondeo

1 Jan Nilsson — Volvo 850
2 Thomas Johansson — BMW 320i
3 'Peggen' Andersson — BMW 320i
4 Mattias Ekstrom — Volvo 850
5 Ulrik Gustavsson — Alfa 155
6 Kari Makinen — Opel Vectra

JUNE 8 — ANDERSTORP
ROUNDS 5 & 6
1 Mattias Ekstrom — Volvo 850
2 Jan Nilsson — Volvo 850
3 Thomas Johansson — BMW 320i
4 'Peggen' Andersson — BMW 320i
5 Stig Blomqvist — Ford Mondeo
6 Ulrik Gustavsson — Alfa 155

1 Jan Nilsson — Volvo 850
2 Thomas Johansson — BMW 320i
3 'Peggen' Andersson — BMW 320i
4 Mattias Ekstrom — Volvo 850
5 Jan Brunstedt — Opel Vectra
6 Kari Makinen — Opel Vectra

JULY 13 — FALKENBERG
ROUNDS 7 & 8
1 Jan Nilsson — Volvo 850
2 Mattias Ekstrom — Volvo 850
3 Stig Blomqvist — Ford Mondeo
4 Anders Soderberg — Ford Mondeo
5 Ulrik Gustavsson — Alfa 155
6 'Peggen' Andersson — BMW 320i

1 Jan Nilsson — Volvo 850
2 Thomas Johansson — BMW 320i
3 'Peggen' Andersson — BMW 320i
4 Stig Blomqvist — Ford Mondeo
5 Jan Brunstedt — Opel Vectra
6 Kari Makinen — Opel Vectra

AUGUST 3 — KNUTSTORP
ROUNDS 9 & 10
1 Jan Nilsson — Volvo 850
2 'Peggen' Andersson — BMW 320i
3 Stig Blomqvist — Ford Mondeo
4 Jan Brunstedt — Opel Vectra
5 Ulrik Gustavsson — Alfa 155
6 Georg Bakajev — BMW 320i

1 Jan Nilsson — Volvo 850
2 Mattias Ekstrom — Volvo 850
3 Stig Blomqvist — Ford Mondeo
4 Kari Makinen — Opel Vectra
5 Ulrik Gustavsson — Alfa 155
6 Jan Brunstedt — Opel Vectra

AUGUST 31 — KARLSKOGA
ROUNDS 11 & 12
1 Jan Nilsson — Volvo 850
2 Thomas Johansson — BMW 320i
3 Stig Blomqvist — Ford Mondeo
4 'Peggen' Andersson — BMW 320i
5 Anders Soderberg — Ford Mondeo
6 Mattias Ekstrom — Volvo 850

1 Mattias Ekstrom — Volvo 850
2 Thomas Johansson — BMW 320i
3 Jan Nilsson — Volvo 850
4 Jan Brunstedt — Opel Vectra
5 'Peggen' Andersson — BMW 320i
6 Stig Blomqvist — Ford Mondeo

CHAMPIONSHIP POSITIONS
1 Jan Nilsson — 249
2 Mattias Ekstrom — 192
3 Thomas Johansson — 159
4 'Peggen' Andersson — 151
5 Stig Blomqvist — 146
6 Jan Brunstedt — 104

DUTCH TOURING CAR CHAMPIONSHIP
1 Duncan Huisman (BMW 320i) — 385
2 Sandor van Es (BMW 320i) — 340
3 Bert Ploeg (Citroen/BMW 320i) — 287
4 Ron Braspenning (BMW 320i) — 282
5 Rob Karst (Renault Megane) — 238
6 Frans Verschuur (Renault Megane) — 235

FRENCH TOURING CAR CHAMPIONSHIP
1 Eric Cayrolle (BMW 320i) — 98
2 Patrick Herbert (BMW 320i) — 76
3 Maurice Perus (Opel Vectra) — 66
4 Bruno Hernandez (BMW 318i) — 51
5 Serge Masson (Peugeot 405) — 35
6 Gilles Duqueine (BMW 318i) — 32

NEW ZEALAND TOURING CAR CHAMPIONSHIP
1 Craig Baird (BMW 320i) — 543
2 Brett Riley (BMW 320i) — 464
3 Peter van Breugel (Nissan Sentra) — 333

SOUTH AFRICAN TOURING CAR CHAMPIONSHIP
(with two rounds to run at Kyalami & Killarney)
1 Giniel de Villiers (Nissan Primera) — 171
2 Duncan Vos (Nissan Primera) — 121
3 Terry Moss (Audi A4) — 114
4 Shaun van der Linde (BMW 320i) — 103

1 Jan Nilsson — Volvo 850
2 Thomas Johansson — BMW 320i
3 'Peggen' Andersson — BMW 320i
4 Stig Blomqvist — Ford Mondeo
5 Jan Brunstedt — Opel Vectra
6 Kari Makinen — Opel Vectra

SWISS TOURING CAR CHAMPIONSHIP
1 Johnny Hauser (Peugeot 405) — 120
2 'Nikko' (Toyota Carina) — 100
3 Daniel Josseron (Opel Vectra) — 74

OTHER TOURING CAR RACES

MARCH 8-9 — ALBERT PARK
AUSTRALIAN GP SUPPORT
1 Jim Richards — Volvo 850
2 Steven Richards — Honda Accord
3 Alan Jones — Audi A4
4 Robert Tweedie — Holden Vectra
5 Justin Matthews — BMW 318i
6 Tony Newman — Peugeot 405

1 Jim Richards — Volvo 850
2 Steven Richards — Honda Accord
3 Geoff Brabham — BMW 320i
4 Paul Morris — BMW 320i
5 Brad Jones — Audi A4
6 Alan Jones — Audi A4

1 Jim Richards — Volvo 850
2 Paul Morris — BMW 320i
3 Geoff Brabham — BMW 320i
4 Steven Richards — Honda Accord
5 Brad Jones — Audi A4
6 Alan Jones — Audi A4

OCTOBER 5 — BATHURST
AMP BATHURST 1000
1 David Brabham/Geoff Brabham - BMW 320i
2 Frank Biela/Brad Jones - Audi A4
3 Jean-Francois Hemroulle/Cameron McConville - Audi A4
4 Jim Richards/Rickard Rydell - Volvo 850
5 Cameron McLean/Jan Nilsson - Volvo 850
6 Peter Brock/Derek Warwick - Vauxhall Vectra
7 Bob Holden/Justin Matthews/Paul Nelson - BMW 320i
8 Brian Bradshaw/Dennis Chapman - BMW 318i
9 Mike Fitzgerald/Jamie Miller - Peugeot 405
10 Julian Bailey/Warren Luff - Honda Accord

OCTOBER 19 — BATHURST
PRIMUS 1000 CLASSIC
1 Russell Ingall/Larry Perkins - Holden Commodore
2 Jim Richards/Steven Richards - Holden Commodore
3 Mark Larkham/Andrew Miedecke - Ford Falcon
4 Craig Baird/Dick Johnson/Steve Johnson - Ford Falcon
5 John Faulkner/Win Percy - Holden Commodore
6 Steve Ellery/Darren Hossack - Holden Commodore
7 Peter Gazzard/Malcolm Stenniken - Holden Commodore
8 Trevor Ashby/Steve Reed - Holden Commodore
9 Ian Luff/Neil Schembri - Holden Commodore
10 Terry Finnigan/Terry Shiel - Holden Commodore

OCTOBER 19 — DONINGTON
TOURIST TROPHY
1 Alain Menu — Renault Laguna
2 Jason Plato — Renault Laguna
3 Rickard Rydell — Volvo S40
4 Frank Biela — Audi A4
5 Yvan Muller — Audi A4
6 Anthony Reid — Nissan Primera
7 Will Hoy — Ford Mondeo
8 Armin Hahne — Volvo S40
9 John Bintcliffe — Audi A4
10 Kris Nissen — Audi A4

Almost 40 years separate these two touring car starts at Snetterton. Above: the 1958 field takes off for a race which was won by Tommy Sopwith's Jaguar, while below Alain Menu leads away on the day he won the '97 title